Using Research Instruments

Clear, accessible and practical, *Using Research Instruments: A Guide for Researchers* introduces the first-time researcher to the various instruments used in social research. It assesses the relative merits of a broad range of research instruments – from the well-established to the innovative – enabling readers to decide which are particularly well suited to their own research.

The book covers:

- Questionnaires
- Interviews
- Content analysis
- Focus groups
- Observation
- Researching the things people say and do

This book is particularly suitable for work-based and undergraduate researchers in education, social policy and social work, nursing and business administration. It draws numerous examples from actual research projects, which readers can adapt for their own purposes. Written in a fresh and jargon-free style, the book assumes no prior knowledge and is firmly rooted in the authors' own extensive research experience.

Using Research Instruments is the ideal companion volume to *The Researcher's Toolkit*. Together they offer a superb practical introduction to conducting a social research project.

David Wilkinson is a Research Fellow within the Work-Based Learning Unit at the University of Leeds. He is the editor of *The Researcher's Toolkit: The Complete Guide to Practitioner Research*, also published by RoutledgeFalmer. David teaches research programmes across a range of undergraduate and postgraduate courses and develops research-based modules for work-based learners.

Peter Birmingham is a Research Officer at the University of Oxford Department of Educational Studies, and a contributor to *The Researcher's Toolkit*. Peter has substantial teaching experience, providing sessions for postgraduate learners on qualitative research methods.

RoutledgeFalmer
Taylor & Francis Group

LONDON AND NEW YORK

Using
Research
Instruments

♦ **A Guide for Researchers**

David Wilkinson
and Peter Birmingham

First published 2003
by RoutledgeFalmer
11 New Fetter Lane, London
EC4P 4EE

Simultaneously published in the
USA and Canada
by RoutledgeFalmer
29 West 35th Street, New York,
NY 10001

*RoutledgeFalmer is an imprint
of the Taylor & Francis Group*

© 2003 David Wilkinson and
Peter Birmingham

Typeset in Sabon by Keystroke,
Jacaranda Lodge,
Wolverhampton
Printed and bound in Great
Britain by TJ International Ltd,
Padstow, Cornwall

*British Library Cataloguing in
Publication Data*
A catalogue record for this book
is available from the British
Library

*Library of Congress Cataloging
in Publication Data*
A catalog record for this book
has been requested.

ISBN 0–415–27279–3

Contents

Illustrations

Illustrations

Figures

Boxes

Acknowledgements

We wish to thank Emma Birmingham for knowing what this book should be about before we ourselves did, and for her constructive comments and suggestions throughout the time we were writing it. David thanks his colleagues in the Work-Based Learning Unit at the University of Leeds for the formal and informal assistance they have given him. Peter thanks his colleagues in the Department of Educational Studies at the University of Oxford for providing such a welcoming environment and one so conducive to work. We both express our thanks also to Anna Clarkson and Louise Mellor at RoutledgeFalmer for their support and encouragement throughout the production of this book.

Permissions

Figure 1.2 reproduced with kind permission of the National Railway Museum, York, UK.

Figure 1.3 reproduced with kind permission of Herts Insurance Consultants plc.

Figures 1.4 and 1.5 reproduced with kind permission of Leeds City Council, Department of Highways and Transportation.

Figures 1.6 and 1.7 reproduced with kind permission of Nick Frost and Nicky Ryder School of Continuing Education, University of Leeds, UK.

Figure 1.8 reproduced with kind permission of Wakefield District Community Safety Partnership – Crime and Disorder Audit Team, who commissioned this work. This work was undertaken by Wakefield Metropolitan District Council (WMDC) Design and Print Services.

Figure 2.2 reproduced with kind permission of the Higher Education Funding Council for England (HEFCE).

Figures 3.1, 3.6, 3.7, 3.8, 3.9, 3.10 reproduced with kind permission of the *Oxford Times*.

Figures 3.2, 3.3, 3.4 reproduced with kind permission of the *Yorkshire Post*.

Figure 4.1 reproduced with kind permission of the Association of American Medical Colleges (AAMC) and Academic Medicine.

Introduction

This book is not a life-saver, but it might just save your sanity and your self-confidence. Whether you are registered on a research methods' course, perhaps as an undergraduate or a postgraduate student, or if, once in work you find yourself having to conduct a modest piece of research as part of your job or study programme, learning about research methods is not easy. We believe tutors and textbooks sometimes underestimate how difficult it can be to get to grips with the bewildering array of options and choices open to the budding researcher. Descriptions of different ways of carrying out research can be baffling, and explanations of when and how to employ particular research instruments to get the job done can be less helpful than they might be. And the longer you study, the more confused you find yourself and the harder it can become to find your feet. If you find yourself in this situation, then this is the book for you.

Dispelling the myth and mystery of social research

Social research is not intrinsically a complicated or thorny enterprise, nor one best reserved for a privileged few professionals or academics capable of undertaking such an intellectually taxing endeavour. But you wouldn't necessarily know this from reading some of the books on the subject. Such books, it seems to us, have been written deliberately to perpetuate the myth and mystery of social research, and to baffle and bamboozle the inexperienced researcher – who really ought to know better and leave it to experts in sociological theory and method. Richard Pring (2000: 57) believes, as we do, that researchers should apply what he calls 'intelligent common sense' to their work rather than rely on 'the silliness which too many writers on . . . research expose us to'.

Other leading researchers have provided us with useful, practical advice: the very first lecture of the research methods' module in Peter's Masters' degree in applied social research was rather unusual, but incredibly helpful. It was a short lecture, perhaps half-an-hour in total, during which the lecturer – an internationally renowned and well-respected professor – made only two points, which he called the two 'central tenets' of social research. The first of these was that 'anything which can go wrong will go wrong', and the second, that 'there are always numerous alternatives'. He wrote both points on the board in large letters, and talked briefly about each in turn. Then he exited the room, leaving the students wondering what on earth they had let themselves in for.

What was the professor getting at with his 'central tenets'? He was dispelling the myth and mystery of social research. Whilst acknowledging that social research has its complex theoretical and philosophical foundations, which can certainly be interesting and rewarding to examine, it is first and foremost a practical, hands-on, activity (or rather a range of alternative activities). What the students learnt from that short lecture was that it doesn't take genius to conduct social research. What it takes is a little thought, a little planning and a lot of practice.

'Anything which can go wrong will go wrong'

With this blunt warning the professor was preparing the class for the reality of research. He was making the point that too many research methods' courses and texts are written along the same lines as recipe books: gather together all the necessary ingredients; follow a short set of instructions; *et voila*, the perfect soufflé! But where do these books deal with inaccurate scales, troublesome ovens, friends coming round at precisely the wrong moment, or the dog licking the bowl before you have transferred the contents into the cake tin? Compare your own untidy, muddled and messy experience of baking with the calm and collected impression of the same process in the recipe book and you are bound to feel deflated, discouraged and even incapable of ever becoming a competent cook.

Anyone who attempts to carry out a small research project can have a similar experience, and feel equally deflated and discouraged afterwards. Research methods' texts tend largely to be written along the same lines, as though the only thing you have to do to ensure your project goes without a hitch is to follow a simple set of instructions. Select a research instrument, do what the author says and everything will be fine. In other words, everything which can go right will go right. But research is simply not like that. There is no point in plunging into your social setting with a fixed recipe. It might be written about as though it takes place in a vacuum, but we all know that this setting is part of the real world, which can be messy and disorganised, and full of challenging, unexpected and problematical twists and turns. We know what unhappy research experiences feel like – it wasn't too long ago that the two of us were learning the ropes ourselves. We remember how depressing it was (and still is) to search out textbooks for reassuring answers as to why things had not gone smoothly, only for them time and again to taunt us by painting a rosy picture of research very far removed from our own frustrating experiences.

We have written this book partly in response to that depressing feeling we remember. That doesn't mean we have written a pessimistic book about problems and failures associated with carrying out research – quite the opposite in fact. But this is a book which accepts that problems and difficulties do occur. So we have tried to write it in a way which anticipates and prepares the reader for unexpected and (at least superficially) unwelcome eventualities. We suggest ways of minimising, bypassing and overcoming difficulties where we can, drawing on what we have learned from our own research experiences. We try to encourage researchers not to lose heart, and instead to see difficulties and dilemmas not as obstacles but as opportunities for refining their research activities, which will be all the more productive and rewarding for overcoming them. If things go wrong (and they probably will), it won't necessarily be because you yourself have done something wrong, so don't worry. 'Anything which can go wrong will go wrong' is a truism, but not one which you should fear. Rather, you should accept it as part of the challenge of research, and try to make the most of it.

'There are always numerous alternatives'

Research instruments are simply devices for obtaining information relevant to your research project, and there are many alternatives from which to choose. The professor's second point was intended to boost students' flagging morale on hearing the first. Basically, if you run into difficulties and your research begins to flounder, that needn't be the end of it. Rather, you should see it as an opportunity for conducting your research differently, by using alternative means. He was impressing upon the class that there is no such thing as *the* definitive method of conducting social research. There is no single research method or instrument *par excellence*. Research is not a 'one-size-fits-all' enterprise. No single research instrument is inherently superior to any other. All can be used well or poorly. Each has its own strengths and weaknesses. Each is more or less appropriate to use in any single research exercise. Whatever your own circumstances, the highest quality social research projects are always those which employ the most suitable methods and instruments in the most thoughtful and careful way.

In our previous text (Wilkinson 2000), we tried to demonstrate that research is not necessarily difficult. It merely involves the adoption of methodical and well-defined procedures and practices. We try in this new book to provide another demonstration of those same sentiments, this time by trying to equip you with a further practical skill. The skill to which we are referring is the ability to assess the relative merits of different research instruments; to determine the suitability of one research instrument over another in relation to any single research project you may be keen to undertake, so that you can clearly say why the advantages of your chosen way of proceeding outweigh those of any alternative.

Another of our aims in writing this book is to help you to acquaint yourself with a range of frequently used research instruments (plus, in the final chapter, a less well-known but refreshingly different alternative) so that on each occasion you will be able to make informed decisions about the instrument best suited to the requirements of your own research.

We provide *definitions* of each research instrument we discuss. We tell you *how* best to use these instruments. We discuss when and why it might be a good idea to use a particular research instrument in your project. We talk about the advantages and disadvantages, the merits and shortcomings, of each. We try to do all these things in as clear, straightforward and accessible a way as possible. Most importantly – and we can't emphasise this enough – each page of what we have written is informed by our own extensive experience of conducting research. What we say is based throughout on what we have learned for ourselves, not only by reading books like this one, but by doing research *for real*. All of the examples of research instruments we use in this book are taken from real-life research projects, and most of them were developed and used by us in projects in which we have been directly involved.

How the book is organised

Social research methods' texts and courses are full of references to the varied continuums which authors have imported from the wider literature in social science and philosophy. These continuums operate as frames of reference, perspectives, paradigms or orientations towards what counts as theory, method, data, explanation, and so on. Some of the most frequently cited are commonly characterised as 'objective' and 'subjective', 'quantitative' and 'qualitative', and 'positivist' and 'interpretivist.' It is not our intention in this book to discuss such weighty matters at length, but if you are interested in debates of this kind we recommend you consult some very clear and accessible expositions by Bryman (1988), Robson (1993) or Pring (2000).

For purely practical rather than philosophical purposes we have organised the chapters of this book along what we have termed a 'researcher–participant control' continuum (see Figure 1.1). This is not the only way we could have ordered the chapters in this book. Indeed, there are many other ways to link each chapter to the next sensibly, from the quantitative nature of questionnaires through to the qualitative character of video analysis, for example. Nevertheless, this is one means of relating separate research instruments that colleagues and students of ours have found particularly helpful, and we hope you find it equally so. At one end of this scale sits the questionnaire. Data collected using this instrument are strictly controlled by the researcher. The researcher sets the questions, determines their order and categorises the responses they generate. Provided respondents complete their questionnaires in the way intended by the researcher, total control of both the instrument and the data remains with the researcher throughout. Research of this nature is entirely *researcher-led*. At the opposite end of the scale sits video-based naturalistic analysis. Unlike research which utilises questionnaires, research of this nature begins without a set of strictly defined research questions. Indeed, part of the research exercise is to determine which questions the data, in the form of video-recordings of a social setting, can be used to solve. This type of research reports the situation under examination as it is actually acted out and demonstrably understood by its *participants*, and not according to some standard imposed by the researcher from the outside looking in. The researcher's role is one of minimum intervention and, once the camera is running, what the research participants do and, therefore, what the data the researcher gathers consists of, are largely – perhaps wholly – out of his or her control. This is research which is entirely *participant-led*. The other research instruments in this text are subject to differing degrees of control and influence by the researcher or his or her research participants.

We begin this text by discussing, in Chapter 1, what is perhaps the most commonly used of all research instruments – the questionnaire. The chapter explores the potential uses of the questionnaire and examines different approaches to setting and posing questions. Limitations are addressed as well as specific design

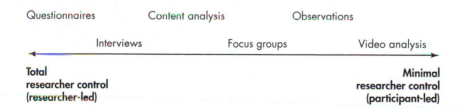

FIGURE 1.1 Researcher–participant control continuum

issues peculiar to this research instrument. Guidance on developing and achieving high response rates is included before we move on to consider the use of web-based questionnaires.

The uses of the research interview are examined in Chapter 2. We begin by defining uses in a research setting before moving on to consider drafting and piloting issues. The types of research interview are discussed along with the use of recording devices in interview situations. As interviews are traditionally resource-intensive, we provide some guidance on sampling and selecting interviewees. We end the chapter by highlighting the steps necessary to successfully conduct a research interview and by examining interview analysis techniques.

Coding data of a textual variety, for example journal articles, written debates and discussions, newspaper pieces, and so on, is covered in Chapter 3, which discusses content analysis. Here, we detail two major approaches commonly used to analyse the content of textual information. Conceptual analysis focuses on a quantitative analysis of information, whereas relational analysis allows relationships between words and concepts to be established and measured.

The focus group – an instrument which has traditionally been used in market research, but which is being increasingly adopted by social researchers – is fully discussed in Chapter 4. There we define this research instrument, discuss its merits, and highlight its potential shortcomings. We also provide a full explanation as to the purposes of a focus group, before guiding you through the process of conducting one for yourself.

Chapter 5 is devoted to an exploration of observation as a research instrument. We begin the chapter by defining observational research and discussing its distinctive character. Much of the chapter is given over to guiding you through planning and conducting your observations. The chapter closes by describing two alternative approaches to recording and analysing your data – a systematic structured approach and a descriptive approach.

Chapter 6 explores the use of video to research the things people say and do. We introduce the video-camera as a research instrument in its own right and provide some explanation of what we term an 'alternative approach to research'. We highlight the relationship of this research instrument to the kind of data it is used to collect, and why it is such a fundamentally-different relationship compared with every one of the other instruments we discuss in this book. We describe in detail the processes involved in the collection, description and analysis of video data, drawing on our own experiences, before moving on to discuss the merits of pursuing video-based research.

Questionnaires

How do we obtain information from individuals regarding their views on particular topics or issues? What is an effective and efficient way of eliciting those views and opinions? We could ask questions of them one by one and record their responses in some way. However, if many people are involved this soon becomes and inefficient and ineffective way of collecting data. In addition, the structure of respondents' answers may not conform to our desired method or an approach to analysis. The questionnaire is the favoured tool of many of those engaged in research, and it can often provide a cheap and effective way of collecting data in a structured and manageable form.

While questionnaires can be very detailed, covering many subjects or issues, they can also be very simple and focus on one important area. A simple yet effective questionnaire is that used by the National Railway Museum in York (Figure 1.2). This form is placed at key locations throughout the museum and its purpose is to seek comments from visitors. This instrument allows the museum to collect, in an effective and efficient way, visitors' views on museum facilities – information of potential value to the future operation of the venue.

Suppose you work in a record store and you'd like to find out which kinds of music some of your younger customers listen to. You think it's a good idea to jot down some questions on some brightly coloured paper (because you've heard that's what youngsters like), and you feel like a proper researcher when you hand out your question sheets in the shopping precinct on a wet Saturday afternoon. However, you are horrified when you receive the responses. Most of those returned (three out of the 400 distributed) are not completed – indeed, over half (two of the three returned) are blank. What have you done wrong? You've discovered that designing an effective questionnaire is no easy task!

Questionnaires can be difficult to design and analyse. Questions posed can be misleading or ambiguous; they may need to be targeted at specific, difficult to reach, groups; and they can create hours, days or weeks of work in analysis. However, a well-planned and well-executed questionnaire campaign can produce rich data in a format ready for analysis and simple interpretation. If correctly managed they can be less resource-intensive than many other research instruments, and they can help gather views and opinions from many individuals, or 'respondents' as they are more commonly termed. Questionnaires have been centrally used to provide an indication of the make-up of society in the UK for centuries in the form of periodic census surveys and are often used by large organisations to establish people's views and opinions on a wide variety of topics.

Why use a questionnaire? Why might they be useful?

We often require information on a range of subjects and to obtain that information we may be required to ask people questions. Questionnaires can be designed and used to collect vast quantities of data from a variety of respondents. They have a number of benefits over other forms of data collection: they are usually inexpensive to administer; very little training is needed to develop them; and they can be easily and quickly analysed once completed.

An effective questionnaire is one that enables the transmission of useful and accurate information or data from the respondent to the researcher. This is a complex process which involves presenting questions in a clear and unambiguous way so that the respondent may interpret them, articulate his or her response and

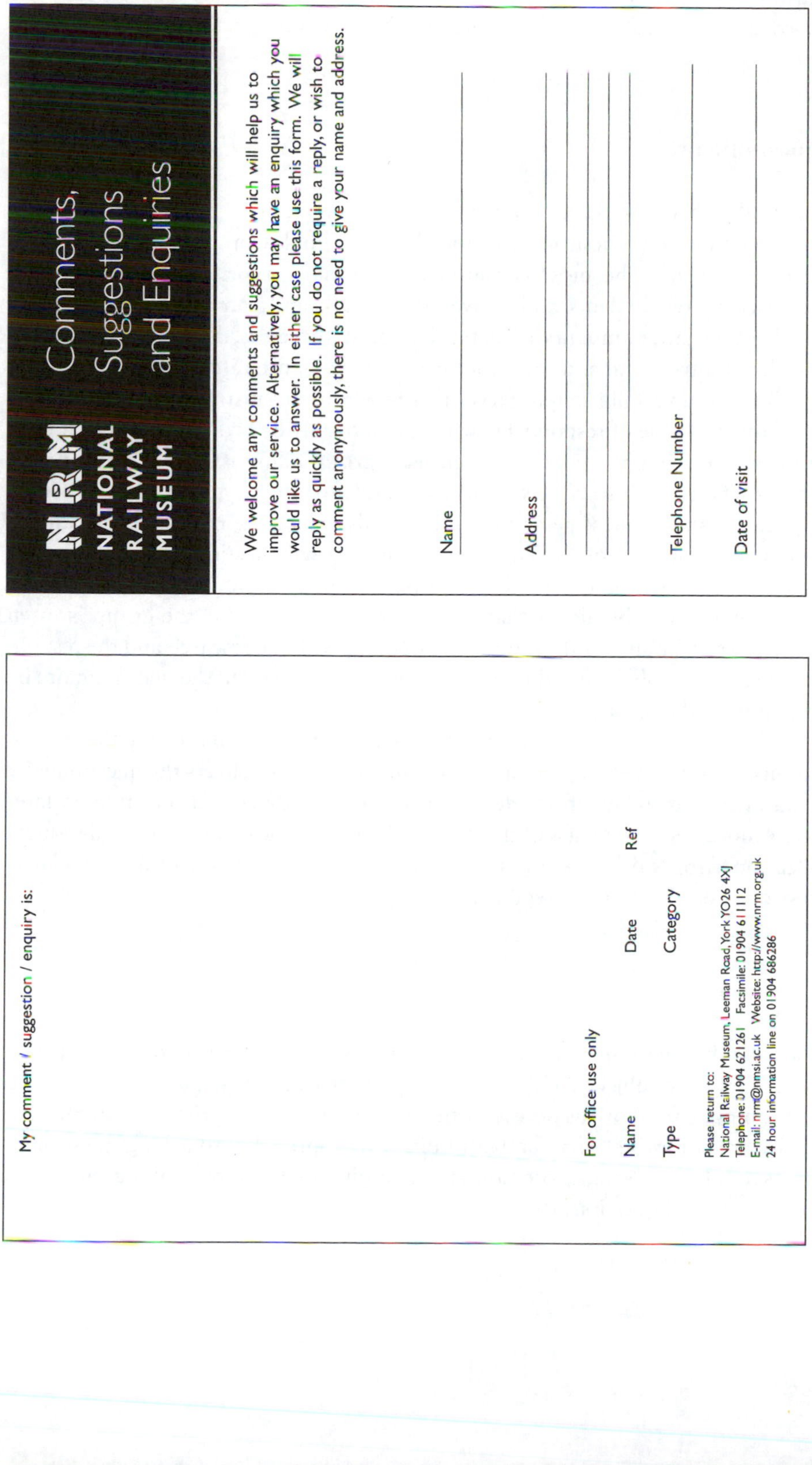

NRM
NATIONAL
RAILWAY
MUSEUM

Comments, Suggestions and Enquiries

We welcome any comments and suggestions which will help us to improve our service. Alternatively, you may have an enquiry which you would like us to answer. In either case please use this form. We will reply as quickly as possible. If you do not require a reply, or wish to comment anonymously, there is no need to give your name and address.

Name

Address

Telephone Number

Date of visit

My comment / suggestion / enquiry is:

For office use only

Name Date Ref

Type Category

Please return to:
National Railway Museum, Leeman Road, York YO26 4XJ
Telephone: 01904 621261 Facsimile: 01904 611112
E-mail: nrm@nmsi.ac.uk Website: http://www.nrm.org.uk
24 hour information line on 01904 686286

FIGURE 1.2 National Railway Museum question form

transmit it effectively to the researcher. Once transmitted, the answers must be recorded, coded and analysed fairly so that they accurately reflect the respondents' views.

Types of questionnaire

Essentially, there are three broad types of questionnaire – the mail survey, the group-administered questionnaire, and the household drop-off survey. The mail survey is, by far, the most common questionnaire type. This instrument is addressed to respondents and delivered by mail, and can be an efficient way of collecting large amounts of data. The mail survey is, however, sometimes considered impersonal and can suffer from low response rates.

The group-administered questionnaire is a useful instrument for collecting data from a sample of respondents who can naturally be brought together for the purpose. For example, we have often used group-administered questionnaires in our own research to collect data from students attending a lecture, teachers in a school and medical personnel in hospitals. This type of instrument allows each member of the group to complete his or her own questionnaire and return it to the researcher on completion. Response rates using group-administered questionnaires can be higher than those for mail surveys, as the group is often assembled specifically for the purpose of assisting with the research and the respondents feel personally involved with the work by being handed the questionnaire by a member of the research team.

The household drop-off survey is a hybrid of the mail and the group-administered survey. Using this approach, the researcher delivers the questionnaire by hand to a member of an identified household for collection at some later date. Among the advantages of this approach are that the drop-off and subsequent collection affords the opportunity for those completing the instrument to clarify questions posed with the researcher.

Types of question

When conducting research we are often interested in collecting data covering a broad range of subjects. Using subtly different questions, and approaches to questioning, can allow us access to the information we require. Questionnaires usually are comprised of a number of different approaches to asking questions – the essential ones being: closed questions, multiple-choice or ranking questions, and open-ended questions (Box 1.1).

BOX 1.1 Question types

Closed questions

Most questionnaires consist of a collection of closed questions. These are questions to which all possible answers are provided. The most often-used form of closed question is the dichotomous question requiring a 'yes' or 'no' response. For example, 'Do you wear glasses?' is a dichotomous question: the respondent either does (responding 'yes') or doesn't (responding 'no') wear glasses.

Multiple-choice questions

Many questionnaires include questions which provide a number of pre-defined responses. This allows the researcher to hold some control over the responses given. However, the construction and piloting of multiple-choice questions usually require careful thought to ensure that all or most responses possible are covered. A typical multiple-choice question would be: *Which of the following are important attributes of an employee? (Please tick all that apply)*

- ☐ Good timekeeping
- ☐ Well developed customer relation skills
- ☐ Good numerical skills
- ☐ Ability to liaise with other staff in other departments.

Open-ended questions

Open-ended questions impose none of the restrictions of closed and multiple-choice questions. They allow for the recording of any response to a question provided by the respondent. The answers to open-ended questions are in no way predetermined – this can make analysis difficult. Each response must be recorded and analysed or coded to reveal the meaning of the response. A typical open-ended question would be: 'Tell us about the area you live in?'

Scale items

Some questions require the respondent to indicate answers according to a pre-defined list or scale, usually ranging from a very positive answer to a very negative answer. There are a number of ways to scale responses to questions. One of the most popular approaches is the Likert scale (published in 1932). This scale, like many others, measures attitudes to set statements put by the questionnaire. The respondent is provided with a scale of possible responses (usually five) to the question – ranging from the attitude measure 'strongly agree' to the exact opposite measure of 'strongly disagree'.

In their work, exploring the public perception of Madeup College, researchers used Likert-type questions in one of their instruments distributed to the residents of Madeup (Box 1.2). This questionnaire asks respondents to tick one area on the rating scale. The questions used in this instrument had been gathered through focus-group work with a select sample of local residents.

BOX 1.2 Likert-type questions

	Strongly agree	Agree	Unsure	Disagree	Strongly disagree
1.1 The College is an important part of the city of Madeup.					
1.2 Even though the Principal of Madeup College has been convicted of fraud, he is still an honourable man.					
1.3 Madeup College should be merged with Clackfax University.					
1.4 The College Coat of Arms is outdated and should be replaced.					
1.5 Madeup College should change its name to the College of Madeup.					
1.6 Disadvantaged learners can succeed at Madeup College.					
1.7 Exams results at Madeup College are . . . made up.					

Other approaches to scaling responses exist and are often used to evaluate products or services. Hertfordshire Insurance Consultants mails postcard-sized questionnaires to its customers seeking views on the services they have received from their insurance consultant (Figure 1.3). The majority of the questions posed are of a Likert-type, requiring the respondent to assign a rating in each instance (others seek comment on improvements to services and request contextual information about the customer). The scale offered ranges from 'excellent', at one end, to 'poor', at the other. Notice that a mid-range (for 'unsure') is not provided: this technique prevents 'questionnaire drift' setting in – the respondent is forced to provide either a positive or a negative view of the statement posed.

Many other scales exist that allow a respondent to rate a statement or question. These include:

How would you judge the quality of the lunch you were served in our restaurant today?
>   Excellent
>   Very good
>   Good
>   Fair
>   Poor
>   Very poor

Compared to other restaurant meals you have had, how was the food we served you?
>   The best I have ever had
>   Better than most other meals
>   OK
>   Worse than most other meals
>   The worst I have ever had

Did our food meet your expectations?
>   Much better than expected
>   Better than expected
>   Slightly better than expected
>   About as expected
>   Slightly worse than expected
>   Worse than expected
>   Much worse than expected

How likely are you to recommend our restaurant to others?
>   Very likely
>   Likely
>   Somewhat likely
>   Neither likely nor unlikely
>   Somewhat unlikely
>   Unlikely
>   Very unlikely

Golden Apple Service Awards

At Herts we are dedicated to providing the highest levels of customer service. To accomplish this, we rely on our people working very hard to meet your needs.

To recognise their achievements, we hold the Golden Apple Service Awards, which are prizes given to outstanding staff members voted for by you, our customers. There are small prizes every month, and a main prize awarded annually. The annual winner will receive a holiday, so they can enjoy a well-earned rest.

To record your views about the person with whom you dealt with recently, please complete and return this FREE reply card.

Please provide your opinion on the following:-

	Excellent	Good	Average	Poor
Your advisor being knowledgeable and enthusiastic?	☐	☐	☐	☐
The main benefits and terms being explained to you clearly?	☐	☐	☐	☐
The paperwork your advisor sent being accurate and correct?	☐	☐	☐	☐

In your opinion, what would be the single most important thing that Herts could do to improve?

....

	Price	Benefits	Service	Recommendation
What was the deciding factor that made you choose Herts?	☐	☐	☐	☐

How would you best describe your buying experience with Herts Insurance?	Excellent	Good	Average	Poor
	☐	☐	☐	☐

Do you own, use, intend to buy any of the following over the next 12 months?	The Internet to purchase	Home Computer	Digital TV	Palm Top PC
	☐	☐	☐	☐

What is your main hobby? ....

FIGURE 1.3 Hertfordshire insurance consultants questionnaire

14

Would you visit our restaurant again?
 Definitely
 Probably
 Possibly
 Uncertain
 Possibly not
 Probably not
 Definitely not

Offering a number of possible responses (such as seven) provides more flexibility to the respondent and affords greater accuracy in recording their views on a given subject. For example, a response of 'definitely' on the above seven-point scale is of more value than 'yes' on a three-point scale (of 'Yes' – 'Unsure' – 'No') because the response is more clearly qualified and reflects what the respondent actually means. It may well be that the 'Yes' box would be ticked by those same respondents ticking 'Definitely', 'Probably' and 'Possibly': only by presenting seven possible responses do we secure a more accurate reflection of the respondent's views.

Routing questions

To enable respondents to complete questionnaires as quickly as possible some designers provide signposts, or routing instructions. These guide the respondent to appropriate areas of the questionnaire. When used effectively they can improve response rate and also ensure the correct elements of the instrument are completed.

Question 9.1   Yes No
Do you watch the TV show The West Wing? ☐ ☐

(If 'No', please go to Question 9.6 below)

Your health

How many cigarettes do you smoke in a day?

Less than 40 Over 40

☐   ☐ ———→ Do you believe this has an effect on your health?

Have you recently reduced the number you smoke?

Design issues and other considerations when using questionnaires

In our experience of using questionnaires we have found that the provision of short and clear instructions to the respondent, at relevant places in the question-naire, can generate more useful and reliable data. If zero is a meaningful answer at some point in your questionnaire, make this clear to those completing. For example, you may be interested to know, as part of a health evaluation programme, how many times your respondents have visited a doctor in the last six months. Without an instruction to the contrary respondents might skip this question if they have not visited a doctor in the preceding six months, and you will lose valuable data as a result. At the analysis stage this will be viewed as a non-response and will have an impact on any claims you make about the data.

Maximising response rates

To maximise response rates consider the use of a covering letter for your questionnaire. This should be short and should explain the research in a clear and understandable way. If data are to be used anonymously, you should state this in your letter, along with information on the accessibility to third parties of your results following completion of the work. A simple and effective covering letter (this one was used for a recent small-scale research project) is provided in Box 1.3).

Another popular way of increasing response rate is to include with the questionnaire a pre-paid return envelope or organise for responses to be returned through a 'Freepost' arrangement. In its Traffic Survey, Leeds City Council included a pre-paid return address on the back of their questionnaire; once the respondent had answered all the questions, they tore off the cover sheet and returned the whole instrument to the Council (Figure 1.4).

Other strategies to increase response rate include offering something to the respondent – such as entry to a prize draw or documentation of the findings from the research.

Many researchers have identified questionnaire design and layout as an important influence on response rates (Jenkins and Dillman 1997; De Leeuw 2001). Some consider that the order of questions can have a favourable (or otherwise) effect on response rate. An American research study indicated that response rate was increased when questions were ordered according to how directly relevant they were to the respondents' working lives (Roberson and Sundstrom 1990).

BOX 1.3 Covering letter for a small-scale research project

Business Ethics

I am undertaking a small research project as part of my studies on a BA (Hons) Business Studies course at the University of Hertfordshire.

The project seeks to gather the views of a number of people in various business organisations in the Hertfordshire area. To do this, a short questionnaire has been developed, which I attach. I would be extremely grateful if you would answer the following questions and return the questionnaire via the address below.

The questionnaire should take no more than fifteen minutes to complete and is anonymous and confidential, so please do not write your name on the paper.

The information you provide will be used for data analysis only. Once the questionnaire is returned, the responses will be aggregated with all the other returns. The data will be analysed using appropriate computer software.

The findings of the project will be available at the end of June 2003. If you would like to receive a summary of my findings please send your address details separately.

Thank you very much for your time.

Darren Hayes
University of Hertfordshire
Final year BA (Hons) student

Ideal questionnaire length and time to complete

How long should a questionnaire be? As a general rule of thumb, a questionnaire should take no more than about twenty minutes to complete. If a respondent is asked to give up more time than this, he or she may abandon part or all of the questionnaire. Respondents may be expected to complete a lengthy questionnaire if there is some identifiable payback for them – but even here a completion time of no more than thirty minutes should be the aim. If the respondent is particularly interested in the subject, he or she might complete the questionnaire over a period of time, working through it one section at a time. However, this increases the amount of time spent in completing the questionnaire; moreover, the respondent's train of thought may be broken and may provide responses that seem disjointed.

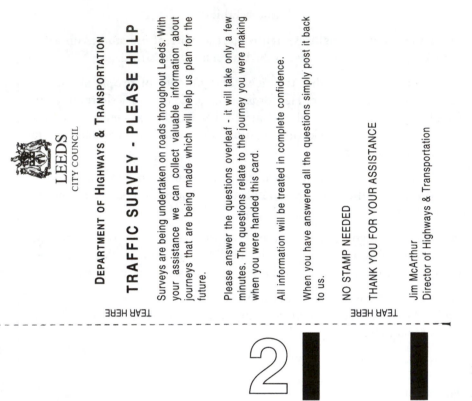

DEPARTMENT OF HIGHWAYS & TRANSPORTATION

TRAFFIC SURVEY - PLEASE HELP

Surveys are being undertaken on roads throughout Leeds. With your assistance we can collect valuable information about journeys that are being made which will help us plan for the future.

Please answer the questions overleaf - it will take only a few minutes. The questions relate to the journey you were making when you were handed this card.

All information will be treated in complete confidence.

When you have answered all the questions simply post it back to us.

NO STAMP NEEDED

THANK YOU FOR YOUR ASSISTANCE

Jim McArthur
Director of Highways & Transportation

TEAR HERE

TEAR HERE

Director of Highways & Transportation
Leeds City Council
Selectapost 6
FREEPOST
Leeds
LS1 1YY

FIGURE 1.4 Increasing response rates – pre-paid return address

Piloting – using a suitable sample group

When designing a questionnaire it is easy to overlook mistakes and ambiguities in question layout and construction. Piloting your instrument with colleagues or a small sample of those who will eventually complete the questionnaire will allow 'fresh eyes' to comment on its suitability and clarity. Usually mistakes are quickly spotted through piloting, and can be rectified relatively easily. In the same way, ambiguous questions can be restated or redeveloped. During the piloting stage, you can observe how long it takes respondents to complete the instrument. Does it fall within the magical twenty minutes' completion time? If not, are there questions you can omit? Are there any open-ended questions that can be converted to closed questions (thereby reducing the amount of time taken to complete them)?

Stratified sampling

When using some of the research instruments outlined in this text (questionnaires in particular) it can be difficult to determine an appropriate sample group or size that is representative of the population in which you are interested. Many research projects take the approach of selecting a stratified sample.

Stratified sampling means establishing your population (such as students) and taking from within that population a sample that represents the whole. For example, if 50 per cent of the student population is female, then 50 per cent of your sample should be female. If 30 per cent of the student population is enrolled on 'business-related courses', then that should be the percentage of your sample of students engaged in 'business-related courses'. In this way, your sample becomes representative of the student population. Sometimes research work is focused upon specific sections of the student population – such as those from a given geographical region or area. Here a stratified sample of all students would be inappropriate, as the research work is focused on a sub-group of that population.

Web-based questionnaires

Many questionnaires are now designed to be completed online, via the internet. They are inexpensive to produce and, if carefully developed and designed, can be automatically coded upon receipt by a specially designed analysis tool (using commonly available database packages). Some work has been conducted on the effectiveness of such approaches to questionnaire design and circulation. Where the questions concern sensitive issues, respondents seem to prefer the standard paper-based instrument. However, computer-assisted self-administered questionnaires produce a higher response rate than their paper-based counterparts (De Leeuw *et al.* 1998).

Coding responses and analysing questionnaire data

Most questionnaires require respondents to register replies to questions by ticking boxes, completing statements, or by providing written replies according to the question type. Answers or responses are coded (i.e. reduced to a number) by the researcher or those responsible for developing the questionnaire. This allows the data from questionnaires to be gathered quickly and then presented in a form more useable for subsequent analysis. It is far easier for a researcher to enter '1' or '2' in a data analysis program than to enter 'pedal cycle' or 'motor cycle'. When coding responses to questionnaires researchers often develop 'coding frames' – instructions reminding them and others which numerical code to use. Essentially, coding provides a kind of shorthand for questionnaire and other research instrument data. The development of appropriate codes and coding should be considered when designing any research instrument. They have been used to good effect by Leeds City Council's Highways and Transportation Department in its recent traffic survey (see Figure 1.5). There, all responses to questions have been designated a unique numerical identifier as prescribed in an accompanying coding frame document (where pedal cycle = 1, motor cycle = 2, cars and taxis = 3, PSV and coaches = 4, light vans and LGV = 5, HGV (two-axle) = 6, and HGV (three-axle) = 7). Under the 'For office use only' column on the far right of the questionnaire, an entry of '1' in box number 6 would indicate the respondent was travelling on a pedal cycle.

Coding in this way makes data analysis much easier for the researcher. To report on the number of respondents travelling by pedal cycle involves tallying, or counting up, all the times the number '1' occurs in the relevant question's coding. A great deal of questionnaire data can be quickly analysed and reported on by using this approach. The process becomes much quicker if computer software is used for entering questionnaire data into a pre-defined database.

It is often useful to obtain an average score in scaled or Likert-type questions in order to compare across questions. By way of an example, let us examine the results from the Madeup College questionnaire discussed above. The responses to questions 1.1–1.3 are provided in Box 1.4. To create an average 'score' for each of these questions we must first convert responses to a numerical value. As 'strongly agree' is the most positive statement, it follows that it should have the highest numerical value, '5'. Conversely, as 'strongly disagree' is the most negative statement, it should have the lowest numerical value, '1'. To calculate the average we multiply the number of responses by the score and divide the total by the

Questions, except No.7, refer to the journey you were making when you were handed this card. Please write your answers opposite.

Write your answers on this half of the card. Tick a box or write in the space provided.

52154

FOR OFFICE USE ONLY

1 In what type of vehicle were you travelling? (Tick one box only).

Pedal Cycle ☐ Motor Cycle ☐ Cars & Taxis ☐ PSV & Coaches ☐

Light Vans & LGV ☐ HGV (2 axle) ☐ HGV (3+ axle) ☐

6

2 How many people were in the vehicle, including yourself?

One ☐ Two ☐ Three ☐ Four or more ☐

7

3 Where were you coming from? (Please give postcode if known, or full address) If you were picking up or setting down a passenger, give that address. If not, please give your own starting point.

Number (or name) and Street ....
District & Town .... Postcode ....

8

4 Where were you going next? (Please give postcode if known, or full address) Please give your final destination, not necessarily where you parked your vehicle. (see next question). If you were picking up or setting down a passenger, give that address.

Number (or name) and Street ....
District & Town .... Postcode ....

15

5 Where did you park or stop your vehicle for the destination given in 4 above?

Address as in 4 above ☐ Car Park Name or Street Name/ Location ....
Town ....

22

a. How long did you park? (minutes) Minutes ....

23

b. How much did you pay? (pence). Pence ....

28

31

6 What was the purpose of the journey between the two addresses given in questions 3 and 4 above? (Tick one box in each column).

FROM ☐☐☐☐☐☐ TO ☐☐☐☐☐☐ Home / Work / Firms Business / Education / Shopping / Other

If other please specify ....

If you were picking up or setting down a passenger, please give that person's purpose.

34

7 If you made a journey yesterday evening between 4.30pm and 6.00pm, please give:

a. The address where you started that journey
Number (or name) and Street ....
District & Town .... Postcode ....

36

b. The address where you finished that journey.
Number (or name) and Street ....
District & Town .... Postcode ....

43

PLEASE TEAR OFF AND POST THIS SECTION (NO STAMP REQUIRED)

FIGURE 1.5 Leeds City Council traffic survey

number of respondents (Box 1.5). Repeating this analysis for each of the questions allows us to compare the positive, or otherwise, reaction of respondents to the questions posed. This may appear a little complicated at first, but there are many computer software packages that will quickly calculate averages for you, once you have accurately coded responses.

BOX 1.4 Likert-type questions – responses

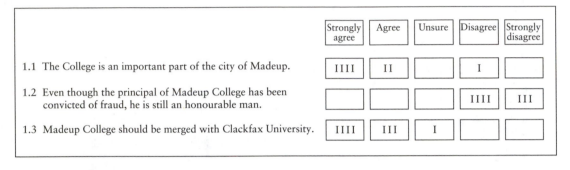

	Strongly agree	Agree	Unsure	Disagree	Strongly disagree
1.1 The College is an important part of the city of Madeup.	IIII	II		I	
1.2 Even though the principal of Madeup College has been convicted of fraud, he is still an honourable man.				IIII	III
1.3 Madeup College should be merged with Clackfax University.	IIII	III	I		

BOX 1.5 Likert-type questions – analysis

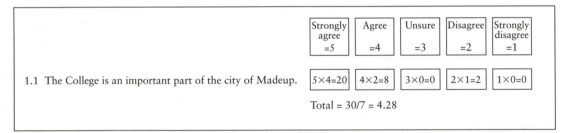

	Strongly agree =5	Agree =4	Unsure =3	Disagree =2	Strongly disagree =1
1.1 The College is an important part of the city of Madeup.	5×4=20	4×2=8	3×0=0	2×1=2	1×0=0

Total = 30/7 = 4.28

In some studies, researchers are interested in the *differences* that occur following certain interventions or events. In their evaluation work, Nick Frost and Nicky Ryden utilised two questionnaires to assess the impact of a parenting programme (Figures 1.6 and 1.7). Using statistical techniques to analyse variances in response, these researchers were able to determine where both positive and negative changes had taken place using sets of questions in both instruments which addressed the same issue or topic. Such techniques as these measure not only the difference in response but also make assertions about the significance or possibility of them occurring by chance. For more detail on statistical measures, please refer to the works listed under 'Further reading – statistical data analysis' at the end of this chapter.

FIGURE 1.6 Questionnaire to parents before parenting programme

UNIVERSITY OF LEEDS
School of Continuing Education

SOUTH LAKELAND FAMILY SUPPORT PROJECT

Questionnaire to parents before parenting programme

We have been asked by Barnardo's to undertake an independent evaluation of the work undertaken by the South Lakeland project. The aim is to help to improve the service for those who use it in the future.

We would be very grateful if you would complete the attached questionnaire.

We would like you to complete a similar from after the last group meeting.

All the information is held confidentially by the researchers and your name will not be used in any reports. We ask you to put your initials on this from so we can compare this one and the one you fill in later.

continued

Please put your initials here   First initial   ❑

                                    Family name initial   ❑

1. Whose idea was it for you to come to the group ?

It was my idea   ❑

It was suggested by a relative   ❑

please say who (husband, mother, etc) _____

It was suggested by a friend   ❑

It was suggested by a professional ❑

please say which profession (health visitor, etc) _____

Someone else ❑

please say who _____

2. Which issues would you like to improve whilst you are coming to the
group ?

Communication with children

VERY IMPORTANT FOR ME   ❑
QUITE IMPORTANT FOR ME   ❑
UNSURE   ❑
NOT IMPORTANT FOR ME   ❑

Finding common interests with children

VERY IMPORTANT FOR ME ❑
QUITE IMPORTANT FOR ME ❑
UNSURE ❑
NOT IMPORTANT FOR ME ❑

Handling family arguments

VERY IMPORTANT FOR ME ❑
QUITE IMPORTANT FOR ME ❑
UNSURE ❑
NOT IMPORTANT FOR ME ❑

Handling children's behaviour

VERY IMPORTANT FOR ME ❑
QUITE IMPORTANT FOR ME ❑
UNSURE ❑
NOT IMPORTANT FOR ME ❑

Setting boundaries and discipline for children

VERY IMPORTANT FOR ME ❑
QUITE IMPORTANT FOR ME ❑
UNSURE ❑
NOT IMPORTANT FOR ME ❑

Helping children with school

VERY IMPORTANT FOR ME ❑
QUITE IMPORTANT FOR ME ❑
UNSURE ❑
NOT IMPORTANT FOR ME ❑

continued

Developing children's play

VERY IMPORTANT FOR ME ❑
QUITE IMPORTANT FOR ME ❑
UNSURE ❑
NOT IMPORTANT FOR ME ❑

Being a step parent

VERY IMPORTANT FOR ME ❑
QUITE IMPORTANT FOR ME ❑
UNSURE ❑
NOT IMPORTANT FOR ME ❑

Being a single parent

VERY IMPORTANT FOR ME ❑
QUITE IMPORTANT FOR ME ❑
UNSURE ❑
NOT IMPORTANT FOR ME ❑

3. How confident do you feel as a parent most of the time ?

VERY CONFIDENT ❑

QUITE CONFIDENT ❑

IT VARIES ❑

NOT VERY CONFIDENT ❑

I HAVE NO CONFIDENCE ❑

I'M NOT SURE ❑

4. I THINK THE BEST THING ABOUT BEING A PARENT IS

5. I THINK THAT THE HARDEST THING ABOUT BEING A PARENT IS

6. IS THERE ANYTHING YOU WOULD LIKE TO ADD ?

FIGURE 1.7 Questionnaire to parents after parenting programme

UNIVERSITY OF LEEDS
School of Continuing Education

SOUTH LAKELAND FAMILY SUPPORT PROJECT

Questionnaire to parents after parenting programme

You may remember filling in a questionnaire for us at the beginning of this programme. We would like you to complete this questionnaire so that we can assess your view of the parenting programme you have recently completed.

You will recall that we have been asked by Barnardo's to undertake an independent evaluation of the work undertaken by the South Lakeland project. The aim is to help to improve the service for those who use it in the future.

All the information is held confidentially by the researchers and your name will not be used in any reports. Please put your initials on the form so that we can compare this to your previous responses.

Please return the questionnaire in the SAE provided. No stamp is required.

THANK YOU FOR YOUR PARTICIPATION

Please put your initials here   First initial   ☐

Family name initial ☐

1. To what extent has the parenting programme assisted you in addressing these issues ?

Communication with children

I feel much more confident   ☐

I feel a little more confident   ☐

I feel about the same   ☐

I feel less confident   ☐

Finding common interests with children

I feel much more confident   ☐

I feel a little more confident   ☐

I feel about the same   ☐

I feel less confident   ☐

Handling family arguments

I feel much more confident   ☐

I feel a little more confident   ☐

I feel about the same   ☐

I feel less confident   ☐

continued

Handling children's behaviour

I feel much more confident   ☐

I feel a little more confident   ☐

I feel about the same   ☐

I feel less confident   ☐

Setting boundaries and discipline for children

I feel much more confident   ☐

I feel a little more confident   ☐

I feel about the same   ☐

I feel less confident   ☐

Helping children with school

I feel much more confident   ☐

I feel a little more confident   ☐

I feel about the same   ☐

I feel less confident   ☐

Developing children's play

I feel much more confident ☐

I feel a little more confident ☐

I feel about the same ☐

I feel less confident ☐

Being a step parent

Not applicable to me ☐

I feel much more confident ☐

I feel a little more confident ☐

I feel about the same ☐

I feel less confident ☐

Being a single parent

Not applicable to me ☐

I feel much more confident ☐

I feel a little more confident ☐

I feel about the same ☐

I feel less confident ☐

continued

2. How confident do you feel as a parent most of the time?

VERY CONFIDENT   ❑

QUITE CONFIDENT   ❑

IT VARIES   ❑

NOT VERY CONFIDENT   ❑

I HAVE NO CONFIDENCE ❑

I'M NOT SURE   ❑

---

3. I THINK THE BEST ASPECT OF THE PARENTING PROGRAMME WAS :

---

4. I THINK THAT THE ASPECT WHICH COULD HAVE BEEN MOST IMPROVED ABOUT THE PARENTING PROGRAMME WAS:

---

5. HOW HAS YOUR PARENTING IMPROVED BECAUSE OF THE PARENTING PROGRAMME?

> **6. WHICH PARENTING ISSUE, IF ANY, YOU WOULD LIKE MORE ASSISTANCE WITH IN THE FUTURE ?**

7. WOULD YOU RECOMMEND ATTENDANCE AT THE PARENTING PROGRAMME TO A FRIEND ?

YES   ☐

NO   ☐

UNSURE   ☐

Please say why

8. IS THERE ANYTHING ELSE YOU WOULD LIKE TO ADD ?

THANK YOU

Limitations

Questionnaires are successfully used in many situations to gather data and infor-mation on a broad range of issues, but they do have application and data-collection limitations, most of which are the product of poor design in the instrument. The major limitations we have found with this much-abused research instrument are discussed below.

Leading questions

When you know your research topic and its issues, it can be difficult to avoid leading questions. After all, you will probably know (through your reading of the literature) far more about the questionnaire's themes than will those completing it. Leading questions are those which provide for only *one* right answer to the question posed. Their wording can suggest that it would be wrong to answer in some particular way, as can be seen from the following:

- Would you prefer to shop on Saturdays if it were more convenient rather than on Sunday (the traditional day of worship)?
- Men have traditionally been the breadwinners in most families. Do you think it is appropriate for women to be breadwinners in some families?
- Even though cannabis has been found to have few adverse side effects, do you still think it should be classified as an illegal drug?

Complicated questions

Your questionnaire may seek to gather a great deal of information, but it would be a mistake to think that complex questions will harvest a greater yield of information. Take, for example, the following question:

> Were there to be a General Election tomorrow, given that the local Labour candidate was known to you, it wasn't raining and there was the chance of receiving a free ride to the polling station, would you vote for the Labour candidate?

Usually, a complicated question like this consists of a number of sub-questions that can be broken down into a number of smaller, more easily understood, questions. Here, the first thing to do is to untangle the questions and ask them separately:

> Were there a General Election tomorrow would you vote? (Please tick the appropriate box below.)

> Do you know the name of your local Labour candidate? (Please tick the appropriate box below.)

Will you vote for the Labour candidate if it is not raining on polling day? (Please tick the appropriate box below.)

Will you vote for the Labour candidate if Labour Party representatives provide free transport to the polling station? (Please tick the appropriate box below.)

Irritating questions

Respondents can find it irritating to be asked to indicate their age. If the information is really required for your work then try to locate the question near the end of the questionnaire. If you consider a question to be potentially irritating then perhaps provide some contextual information in the questionnaire as to why this particular question is necessary.

Ambiguous or unclear questions

Try to be as clear as possible in wording your question. Those completing your questionnaire are unlikely to be as familiar with your core research topic as you are yourself. Be specific wherever possible in posing your questions. Often questionnaires include statements of the type:

Do you regularly use a gym?

The person completing your questionnaire may be confused as to what this means. How often is 'regularly'? Some respondents may go to the gym to use the sauna or for some beauty therapy, while others may visit the gym for a workout. Both are 'uses' of the gym, but are they providing the information you require?

It can be useful to break the question down:

Do you use a gym? (Please tick the appropriate box below.)

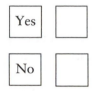

If 'Yes', do you visit a gym *at least* three times per week? (Please tick the appropriate box below.)

What about the enquiry? There are many other ways to ask ambiguous or unclear questions.

Where do you use the internet? (Please tick one box from the list below.)

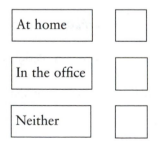

This question assumes the respondent uses the internet in only *one* of the places listed. What should the respondent do if he or she uses the internet at home *and* in the office? Had you asked respondents to tick only one box and they ticked both the 'at home' and 'in the office' boxes, how would you analyse this response? Additionally, what should those respondents do who use the internet but do not use it at home or in the office, but while studying at the local college or university? One way of overcoming this potential problem would be to insert a third option, 'Other', to accommodate non-specified locations for using the internet.

Even the experts get it wrong sometimes. In research work examining the wording of questions posed in large national health surveys in the USA, ambiguities were found in a number of the key questions (Box 1.6). The research work indicated that thorough piloting and testing of questions may have weeded out poorly defined and ambiguous questions from the questionnaires. One question asked respondents what was the average number of days per week on which he or she ate butter. At first glance, this question might seem quite clear, but the research established, through testing the questions with a number of respondent groups and observing their reactions and comments, that many respondents were unclear as to whether the question included margarine consumption as well. A clearer question was developed, and it was found that butter consumption was lower than originally thought.

BOX 1.6 An unclear question (taken from Fowler 1992)

Original question:
What is the average numbers of days each week you have butter?

Revised question:
The next question is about butter. Not including margarine, what is the average number of days each week you have *butter*?

Too many open-ended questions

Questionnaires, in the main, should be used for focused and direct questions. It may be useful to allow a number of open-ended questions into the questionnaire, though care should be taken here. Too many open-ended questions force those completing your questionnaire to put more effort into their answers. For that reason, a number of questionnaires place open-ended elements towards the end of the instrument, allowing respondents to add any further comment he or she think appropriate to the subject. This is shown in the instrument (Figure 1.8) developed by Wakefield District Council as part of its data-gathering exercise relating to community safety.

YOUR SAY IN OUR PRIORITIES FOR COMMUNITY SAFETY

Please take a few minutes to complete and return this form to the Freepost address given - no stamp needed. Your views matters. Together we can be even stronger.

What do YOU think?
The Partnership is keen to know your views and, in particular, if you feel there are others areas of crime and disorder it should address.

Please return this slip 'FREEPOST' to reach us by 5 January, 2002. Send it to:
Community Safety Audit,
The Citizen,
Freepost NEA5394
Town Hall,
Wakefield WF1 2BR

THANK YOU FOR YOUR HELP!

1 Does the information provided in the leaflet match your own experience or perceptions of crime in your area?

Yes ☐   No ☐

If no, were you expecting
More crime? ☐   Less crime? ☐

2 What should our priorities be for tackling crime and disorder? Indicate your five priorities by writing 1 to 5 in the boxes (1 = top priority, 5 = lowest)

Alcohol abuse ☐	Anti-social behaviour amongst adults ☐
Burglary ☐	Domestic violence ☐
Drug related crime ☐	Fear of crime ☐
Graffiti and vandalism ☐	Homophobic crime ☐
Racial crime ☐	Road safety ☐
Theft from shops and businesses ☐	Traffic offences (ie speeding) ☐
Youth crime & disorder ☐	
	Arson ☐
	Drug abuse ☐
	Fly-tipping, pollution ☐
	Neighbour nuisance ☐
	Safety on public transport ☐
	Vehicle crime ☐

Please tell us about any other issues or make any comments about the progress so far.

3 To ensure we can relate these views to the area in which you live, please tell us a little about yourself. This information will not identify you

Postcode ☐

Gender ☐

Do you have a disability? ☐

Age   0-10 ☐   11-16 ☐   17-24 ☐   25-34 ☐   35-44 ☐   45-54 ☐   55-64 ☐   65+ ☐

Ethnicity   White ☐   Mixed ☐   Asian/Asian British ☐   Black/Black British ☐   Chinese/Other Ethnic Group ☐

FIGURE 1.8 Use of open-ended elements in questionnaires

Reasons to use questionnaires

- Questionnaires can facilitate the collection of vast amounts of data with minimal effort.
- Well-designed questionnaires can allow relationships between data to be identified. They are particularly useful for showing relationships with data that are easily quantifiable.
- Questionnaires protect respondent anonymity: they can be distributed and returned confidentially and without the respondent ever being identified.
- As research instruments, questionnaires can be used time and time again to measure differences between groups of people. They are reliable data-gathering tools.
- If coded in an appropriate way, they can enable analysis to be conducted extremely quickly and with low error rates.
- Unlike some other instruments (such as unstructured interviews) the researcher retains control over the research, directing how the topic is approached and guiding the respondents to discuss the issues selected.

Reasons not to use questionnaires

- Ease of production and distribution can result in the collection of far more data than can be effectively used.
- Questionnaires are everywhere, competing for respondents' time. Lack of adequate time to complete the instrument may result in the return of superficial data.
- Lack of personal contact (if the questionnaire is mailed) may mean that response rates suffer, necessitating the expense of follow-up letters, telephone calls and other means of 'chasing' the respondent.

Key textbooks focusing on developing and using questionnaires

For those new to research

Gillham, B. (2000a) *Developing a Questionnaire*, London: Continuum Books, 89 pp., indexed. Brief section on suggested reading.

This brief text forms part of a series of such books focusing on key skills required of researchers as they conduct their work. The Introduction states that the text is designed for use by those with no prior knowledge of questionnaire design, and the writing style reflects this. Bill Gillam, a psychologist based at the University of Strathclyde, covers the fundamental aspects of questionnaire design. The benefits of using questionnaires are discussed, and there is advice on improving returns, analysis and presentation of findings.

For the intermediate researcher

Cohen, L., Manion, L. and Morrison, K. (2000) *Research Methods in Education*, London: RoutledgeFalmer, 446 pp., indexed. See Chapter 14: Questionnaires.

In this fifth edition of their popular and user-friendly text, Cohen, Manion and (more recently) Morrison detail the major stages of questionnaire design and execution. Chapter 14 offers guidance on how to plan questionnaires effectively, on ethical issues, layout, piloting and processing questionnaire data. For the developing researcher, this chapter provides particular assistance with devising appropriate and clear questions for inclusion in a variety of projects, drawing from a wide range of question types.

For the expert

Oppenheim, A. N. (1992) *Questionnaire Design, Interviewing and Attitude Measurement*, London: Continuum Books, 290 pp., suggested reading, indexed.

This textbook, first published in 1966, has been substantially rewritten to incorporate recent developments in questionnaire design, use and data analysis, and has been reprinted nine times since 1992. It is considered a key text on most major research courses, and is heavily used by those engaged in market research. Drawing on his own substantial record of research activity, Dr Oppenheim provides assistance on effective survey design and gives a historical commentary on survey/questionnaire development. Essential and relevant theories are discussed in a user-friendly way. Figures, tables and charts are used throughout the text to emphasise or clarify points. Of particular use to any researcher are the detailed notes and guidance relating to question design and wording, and attitude scaling and measurement. A comprehensive text, it covers a range of other important subjects, including the statistical analysis of data generated by questionnaires and the importance of efficient data processing.

Further reading – statistical data analysis

Brown, A. and Dowling, P. (1998) *Doing Research/Reading Research: A Mode of Interrogation for Education*, London: Falmer Press. See Chapter 2: Dealing with quantity.

Howell, D. C. (1996) *Fundamental Statistics for the Behavioral Sciences*, Newbury Park, CA: Sage.

Kanji, G. K. (1999) *100 Statistical Tests*, London: Sage.

Interviews

Interviews are not an easy option. They are often likened to a conversation between two people, though a competent researcher knows that he or she are more than this: he or she require orchestrating, directing and controlling to varying degrees. Interviews 'involve a set of assumptions and understandings about the situation which are not normally associated with a casual conversation' (Denscombe 1998: 109).

Interviews have long been used in research as a way of obtaining detailed information about a topic or subject. Often interviews are used where other research instruments seem inappropriate: for instance a recent study, in which we were involved, exploring basic literacy skills among adults, interviews were used because it seemed inappropriate to ask respondents who had limited literacy skills to complete lengthy questionnaires. In many situations the use of a research interview rather than, say, a questionnaire can be an indicator of the greater importance attached to the research topic. Questionnaires are relatively inexpensive to produce, circulate and analyse. The research interview is far more resource-intensive. It requires the researcher to elicit information from respondents on a one-to-one basis. Interviews can last for longer than an hour and can produce vast amounts of data. It has been said that while other instruments focus on the surface elements of what is happening, interviews give the researcher more of an insight into the meaning and significance of what is happening.

As with other research instruments, there are a number of stages to developing and effectively using interviews (Box 2.1).

BOX 2.1 Stages in developing and using interviews

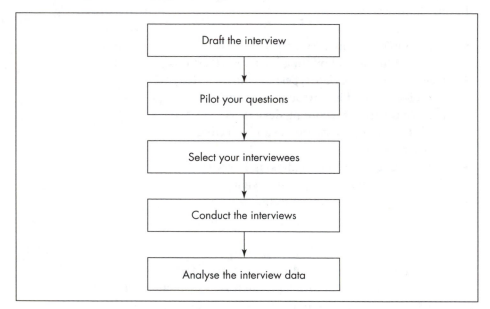

Draft the interview

Pilot your questions

Select your interviewees

Conduct the interviews

Analyse the interview data

Draft the interview

The interview development process begins by broadly indicating the questions which you'd like to ask. The number, type and format of your questions will be informed by the level of structure to be imposed on the interview. Interviews are traditionally less structured than other research instruments, such as questionnaires. However, three models for interviews exist: the unstructured interview; the semi-structured interview; and the structured interview.

The unstructured interview

The unstructured interview is a very flexible approach. Areas of interest are established by the researcher but the discussion of issues is guided by the interviewee. This allows some control over the interview for both interviewer and interviewee. However, unstructured interviews can be difficult to plan (in terms of the time to be given to the event), they are difficult to 'steer' if the discussion gets away from the key subject matter, and they can prove extremely difficult to analyse.

The semi-structured interview

There is less flexibility with the semi-structured interview. The interviewer directs the interview more closely. More questions are predetermined than with the unstructured interview, though there is sufficient flexibility to allow the interviewee an opportunity to shape the flow of information.

The structured interview

Some see the structured interview as no more than a questionnaire that is completed face-to-face. The interviewer has control over the order of questions, all of which are predetermined. There is an element of predictability to the structured interview which allows the event to be timetabled with some precision (an interview scheduled to last an hour will usually do so). Unlike the other models for interviews, the structured interview may provide an easier framework for analysis.

It can be difficult to accurately distinguish between unstructured and semi-structured interviews, and the criteria for each may appear merely academic. However, there is agreement that unstructured interviews are controlled and directed by the interviewee, whereas semi-structured interviews have predefined areas for discussion. In the semi-structured interview the format and ordering of the questions are informed by the ongoing responses of the interviewee to the questions posed. Figure 2.1 on page 46 provides the transcript of an unstructured interview with a headteacher on the subject of free school meals.

This interview transcript highlights a major disadvantage of the unstructured interview – control lies with the interviewee. From the eighty-five minutes of interview time, perhaps the most significant data, from the researcher's point of view, came in the last few minutes. Sometimes interviewees have subjects or 'agendas', other than those agreed, that they want to talk about. It can take time and considerable patience to encourage them to answer your questions or discuss the

---

Research project exploring the provision of free school meals in a sample of secondary schools in north-west England

Location   Headteacher's office, Fieldwork Secondary School, Petersfield

Interviewer   Alan Fishgard (AF)

Interviewee   Headteacher George Mapplewell (GM)

Date   10 January 2003

Interview start time 1:55 p.m.

Interview end time   3:30 p.m.

AF: Mr Mapplewell, as you are the headteacher of a busy secondary school, I'd like to thank you for giving up some of your time to speak to me today. As I indicated in my letter, I'd appreciate your views on the subject of the eligibility, provision and take-up of free school meals. You have kindly agreed to give up half-an-hour of your day to speak to me on this subject. I'd like to begin by asking you to provide some context for me, if you would. Tell me a little about free meal provision at Fieldwork School.

GM: Yes, of course, Alan. Now. Free school meals you say? Well there aren't many learners in this school who actually have them – I prefer to call them 'learners', and not 'children', as its part of the progressive attitude we have here at Fieldwork. Our learners really appreciate that. I was saying only the other day, to Helen (the school secretary), that if you treat them like *learners* then they act like learners.

(George Mapplewell continues to discuss the 'progressive' nature of the school and despite gentle reminders from the interviewer, he does not return to the subject of free meals for at least an hour. That part of the transcript has been deleted as it has no relevance to the subject matter)

GM: About ten years ago approximately 30 per cent of learners in my school were eligible for free meals. Of these about 20 per cent came from the local authority housing estate next to the school. Of course, these houses were condemned relatively recently as they have structural problems caused by the subsidence in the area following heavy coal mining in the 1950s and 1960s. Now the school draws its population from the very affluent areas to the north and south of the school. In the main free meals' eligibility nowadays goes to the learners who are from one-parent families.

FIGURE 2.1 Interview transcript – provision of free school meals project

topic of your research. Preparing themes or question areas may help. In any interview – structured, semi-structured or unstructured – it is important for the interviewer to prepare a list of key questions to be covered so that important issues are not overlooked and the interview follows a logical progression.

In a recent study exploring the roles and functions of technical staff in the UK's higher education sector, researchers based at Evidence Ltd prepared a schedule for interviews to be held with university staff members. The planned interviews were formal events and the schedule assumed a structured approach with a common interview outline, tailored to stated groups, but with room for some exploration of points as they arose throughout the course of the interview. This facilitated an increase in the comparability of the work of technical staff at different universities and ensured that key issues were covered methodically and equally (see Figure 2.2 on pages 48–51).

It is important at the drafting stage to clarify both the number and type of questions you will ask and how they will be sequenced during the interview. A primary purpose of the interview is to collect data and information you could not easily gather elsewhere. They are resource-intensive events in terms both of your time and, more importantly, of your interviewee's time. As a result, each question you ask must be necessary and clearly phrased in order to gather as much information as possible.

Some interview questions address more sensitive and controversial subjects than do others, and a useful way of approaching the development of such questions is to apply a funnelling technique to the sequencing of the topics covered by the interview. In all good interviews, questions will be clustered or grouped around themes or issues and these broad areas of research interest will be communicated to the interviewee at the beginning of the interview session. Using the funnelling technique, questions will move from general opening enquiries to more specific and focused questioning. This approach allows interviewees to relax into the interview and helps them to develop a logical and comfortable progression to their responses.

Finally, at the drafting stage, a decision should be made concerning how interviews will be recorded. Researchers have for many years made considerable use of audio-recorders during interviews – for one obvious yet fundamentally important reason: audio-recorded interviews can be transcribed. Conversations are fleeting things, in which an enormous and wide-ranging amount of information can be shared in a short period of time. Interviews are no different. No matter how attentive and meticulous you are as an interviewer, you will never be able to include everything in your write-up of the interview if you rely on memory and a pad of hastily scribbled notes. Transcriptions, on the other hand, are records of every word you and your interviewees say and, as such, they are infinitely more reliable than any notes, quotes, remarks and summaries you might jot down during an interview.

FIGURE 2.2 Highly skilled technicians in higher education research project

evidence

HIGHLY SKILLED TECHNICIANS IN HIGHER EDUCATION

Introduction

This major project has been commissioned by the Higher Education Funding Council for England. It is being conducted by Evidence Ltd whose consultants have substantial experience of working with the HE sector on a number of projects. The work is being carried out between November and December 2001 and the purpose of the work is to illuminate the role and function of the highly skilled technician. The project has two stages or phases (see below). In order to minimise the burden on institutions, we anticipate completing both phases within a one-day site visit. However, given the rich and varied nature of the data it may be necessary to negotiate further access with case study institutions.

Themes and questions

Technicians are an overlooked, but key, group in the higher education research system. The study is designed to fill this information gap. It is not concerned with developing policy recommendations.

Data will be collected primarily through a series of site visits to a structured sample of higher education institutions (HEIs) and other organisations. This note indicates the broad themes and indicative questions involved. Each site visit comprises two elements.

1 Institutional overview

Participants in this element of the study include HEI representatives able to address institutional policy and procedures, statistics and management issues with regard to technicians. We predict that these issues will be best addressed through a series of individual interviews with a representative from each of the following areas of responsibility:

♦ senior management
♦ human resources
♦ finance/research contracts
♦ a trades union

Interviews will be semi-structured and grouped around a number of themes relevant to the specialist areas of responsibility of the HEI representatives:

Defining the highly skilled technician

♦ How does the HEI identify–classify–reward its highly skilled technicians.
♦ What specific skills are involved?
♦ How are technicians with these skills distributed and deployed across the HEI?

Qualifications, training and career progression

♦ What are the main qualifications held by highly skilled technicians?
♦ What are the main recruitment 'pools' for technician roles?
♦ What are the main entry requirements to technician grades?
♦ What training/staff development is required in order to progress to highly skilled roles?
♦ How is training provided – e.g. at what levels is training/development/acquisition of additional qualifications managed (university, department, off-site, etc.)?
♦ What are the resource implications of continuing professional development for technicians (in terms of technician and other staff time/money)?
♦ Are career progression routes changing and, if so, how?
♦ Are there any specific gender issues involved (differences in terms of roles, training, progression, contracts, etc.)?
♦ Are there any other equal opportunity issues, e.g. disability?

Recruitment and retention

♦ To what extent does the technician labour market interface with other organisations (e.g. schools/colleges, private research organisations, etc.)?
♦ How difficult is it to attract technicians to HEI employment?
♦ Is retention of highly skilled staff problematic and, if so, why?
♦ Are there any particular problems with conditions of employment – proportions on permanent/fixed term contracts, continuity of contracts?
♦ Is casualisation an issue?

Funding

♦ What income streams pay for technicians?
♦ How does the HEI apportion this resource, i.e. how are technicians costed into research proposals?
♦ Are current approaches to the funding of technicians sustainable?

continued   **49**

Management information

♦ What systems are deployed for classifying and accounting for technician grade staff?

♦ What is the balance between the HEI and its resource centres in handling and developing information on technicians?

♦ Are there any specific information gaps?

Future scan

♦ What are the anticipated problems/opportunities in relation to highly skilled technicians over the next decade?

♦ On a UK scale, are there any particular concerns about the ability of the HE research base to maintain its technical competence in the future?

Interviewee needs from this study

Are there any specific issues you would like to see being addressed through this study?

2 The research process: roles and relationships

The focus for the second element of the study is those staff who are more directly involved with the research process. We include here principal investigators and the highly skilled technicians involved in the research team, specifically those technicians (rather than other support staff) who provide some expertise/input into the research process and who, often, work alongside identified researchers in laboratory settings.

For our case study work it is important that we identify *two* separate research groups (i.e. in different research disciplines) for interview. For each group we would wish to interview a small number of people, to include the principal investigator and one or two highly skilled technicians. As in the previous section, all interviews will be conducted with individuals. Where time permits, however, it may also be possible to conduct a number of shorter group interviews with relevant postdoctoral research assistants (PDRAs) and postgraduate research students (PGRS) who are also involved in carrying out some technical functions for the research group(s) involved.

The purpose of the interviews will be to explore the broad themes (identified above) directly with those responsible for carrying out the roles. These interviews will necessarily be only lightly structured. The principal aims are to understand the technicians' settings or environments, their roles and relationships with those they work with and issues concerning training and development.

The intention is to build up detailed answers to the following indicative questions:

- ♦ How are the roles of highly skilled technicians actually carried out (this is more important to us than finding out about specific jobs)?
- ♦ How do technicians' roles overlap with others involved in research, e.g. RAs, PDRAs, PGRSs?
- ♦ How are relationships and roles between technicians and academics structured and conducted?
- ♦ What changes are taking place in roles?
- ♦ How do these break down into various sub-units?
- ♦ Are there substantial differences between disciplines
- ♦ Are there institutional/local procedures for appointing technical staff?
- ♦ In this unit/department what is the typical profile of technicians (age, gender, education/training)?
- ♦ How much control do technicians have over their work?
- ♦ What are technicians' key contributions to the research process?
- ♦ Are technicians able to direct their own training/development requirements?
- ♦ Who determines technicians' continuing development?
- ♦ What forms do development programmes take?

David Smith
Jonathan Adams
October 2001

Source: Evidence Ltd

There is no reason why a video-camera cannot be used in the same way. Video-recordings contain an audio track, which means interviews recorded on video can be transcribed equally as effectively as audio-recorders. The disadvantage posed by the camera's size and its potential to be intrusive in an interview situation is offset by at least three advantages we can see (summarised in Box 2.2). First, we have conducted one-to-one interviews during the course of our own research where it has been important not only to record what our subjects are saying, but also to be able to see them as they say it. In other words, the video-camera is able to capture the visual components of an interview, for example an interviewee pointing to a graph, demonstrating a computer program, taking the interviewer through a PowerPoint presentation, or discussing the layout of the room in which the interview is taking place, all while he or she is talking. Second, we have found it a lot easier to transcribe focus-group interviews, and then to analyse the transcripts, when we've been able to see, as well as hear, who is talking. It can be a lot more difficult to discern whose comments are whose if you are working solely from an audio track. Third, psychologists are fond of telling us that a very great deal of human communication is non-verbal. If that is the case, who knows what you might miss if you rely on audio-recorded interviews alone? In light of these examples we can begin to see the usefulness of video-cameras in research.

BOX 2.2 Advantages of using video to record interviews

> ♦ Records what is being said with visual cues.
> ♦ Can clearly identify who is speaking in a group.
> ♦ Makes it possible to observe and make note of body language.

Pilot your questions

No research instrument is perfect. You can begin to identify and correct imperfections (before its too late) by piloting, or testing out, your questions with a select few people in order to establish their clarity. Many researchers carefully craft their interview questions, structuring the instrument around key themes or subject areas – but they fail to pilot the questions they intend to use. Piloting is crucial. It assists in eliminating ambiguous questions as well as in generating useful feedback on the structure and flow of your intended interview. As with other research instruments, interview questions should be easy to understand.

Select your sample interviewees

Because interviews take longer to plan, conduct and analyse than do some other research instruments, extra care must be taken when selecting the sample group of interviewees. Even the most competent and hardworking of researchers cannot expect to interview all those associated or involved with the topic under scrutiny. Every interview conducted of, say, an hour's duration will take at least twice that time to transcribe; will take considerable time to set up; and will usually involve the researcher visiting the interviewee on their 'home turf' to conduct the interview. For these reasons, your sample of interviewees must be representative – if you are to make generalisations from the data they provide – and sensible. Your central research question or questions should help you to decide how many interviewees you will require and who you should interview. If you are conducting more than one interview in the same organisation, it is accepted that these should take place from the 'top down' i.e. interviews with heads of departments or sections usually precede those with employees who report to them.

Conduct the interview

The physical organisation of your interview setting is an important part of the interview process. Very formal interview situations tend to position the interviewer in front of the interviewee – often with a desk between them. However, this approach can appear confrontational and may intimidate the interviewee (although it has also been used on occasion as a tactic to intimidate the interviewer!).

Less formal seating arrangements in interview situations tend to put both parties at ease. The most common seating plan consists of interviewer and interviewee sitting alongside each other, with any recording device (such as video- or audio-recorder) discreetly placed so as not to intimidate or distract the interviewee. Note-taking can slow down the interview and distract the interviewer unless restricted to brief notations or summaries for later elaboration. It is also good practice in interview situations for the researcher to begin by introducing him or herself, outlining the purpose of the interview and its intended format and structure. The interviewer should indicate how the data from the interview will be used and whether anonymity will be preserved.

Open-ended questions encourage the interviewee to provide more information than do closed questions. Some of the examples of interview schedules in this chapter use open-ended questions – often beginning with such words as 'what', 'how', 'tell me', or 'can you indicate' rather than restrictive words which close possible responses, such as 'how many', 'when' or 'what type'.

It is important for the interviewer to provide the interviewee with comforting signs or acceptance cues. These can enhance the interview and generally encourage the interviewee to provide information. Such cues include nodding the head to indicate understanding and interest in the interviewee's response, and adopting an attentive posture by sitting straight and leaning slightly forward. It also encourages response if the interviewer maintains eye contact with the interviewee. This is generally interpreted as interest in what the interviewee is saying, communicating a focus on their views and opinions. However, common sense should prevail here, as too much eye contact (more than about 50 per cent of the time) can be interpreted as staring. (Box 2.3 offers two more suggestions for interviewers.)

To ensure effective communication has taken place in relation to a topic or question, it can be useful for the interviewer to restate part or all of the interviewee's response. Restatement can clarify what has been said – particularly if specialised language or terminology have been used in the initial response – as well as prompting the interviewee to expand or elaborate on what he or she has said.

Silence in an interview can be deafening. Many novice researchers feel a need to fill a silence in an interview. Experience has taught us to attempt to use silence

BOX 2.3   Two 'tricks of the trade' for interviewers

♦   Sometimes respondents find it difficult to recall certain events or actions in which they were involved. In these situations the researcher can use certain memory cues to probe the respondent. When focusing on a specific issue or concern, use a few introductory or context questions. This allows the respondent to be brought back to the situation in which the researcher is interested. These context or 'scene-setting' questions are followed by the 'real' question. For example: 'How often do you shop for food essentials? Where do you usually shop for these? Last time you went shopping did you buy coffee? (Now the key question) Which brand of coffee did you buy most recently?'

♦   In standard training, interviewers are often instructed to probe once after an initial 'Don't know' response, or when a respondent hesitates in choosing the appropriate response. Often, given suitable time to reflect on the question, a respondent can provide more precise, and therefore more valuable, information.

as an aid to gathering more information. A silence following the interviewer's question allows the interviewee to collect thoughts and begin to frame an answer. This will be the first time they have heard the question, and they will need time to interpret it and respond. Silence can be usefully employed also when an interviewee has given a limited or incomplete answer to the question posed. If carefully used, silence can encourage an extended response.

When all question areas have been covered, it is necessary to draw the interview to a close. This provides an opportunity for the researcher to paraphrase what has been said and discussed (allowing the interviewee to add further information or correct inaccuracies in the interviewer's interpretation of responses). It is also common practice to thank the interviewee and offer to provide a written summary/report (if resourcing allows) of the interview. More suggestions regarding the efficient conducting of interviews are given in Box 2.4.

Many of the points on p. 55 were put to excellent effect in a recent study of mentoring activities in UK schools. Consultants from Research in Action were commissioned to assist with the evaluation of a number of schemes designed to provide mentoring support to disaffected learners. The consultants were keen to obtain the views of a selection of key stakeholders within each programme: the mentors, the learners and the teachers. The research team decided that the best way to obtain views and perceptions on the usefulness of the various schemes was to conduct structured interviews with individuals from each group of participants.

BOX 2.4   Tips for interviewers

> To help the flow of the interview, and to put the interviewee at ease, there are a number of actions a good interviewer should take:
>
> 1   Tell the interviewee who you are (if you haven't already introduced yourself by letter or telephone for example).
> 2   Say why the interview is taking place and explain the importance of the interview to your research.
> 3   Before you proceed with your questions, ask the interviewee if she has any questions about the research.
> 4   If you intend to take notes or tape-record the interview, ask the interviewee's permission.
> 5   It is often useful to share the main points you have noted with the interviewee at the end of the interview. This allows the interviewee to clarify points or make further comment.

Figure 2.3 provides the interview schedule used for mentors, and Figure 2.4 that used for learners.

The examples below of interview schedules indicate how questions are structured according to the interviewee, often being based on what we expect them to know. We can see that the learners' questions are brief and to the point whereas the questions posed to the mentor cover more issues and are less strictly focused. The interviewer is also instructed (in the learner schedule) to mention, wherever possible, the name of the mentoring scheme so that the learner can identify more directly with the question and supply an answer based on experience.

Telephone interviews

Face-to-face interviews are the most expensive form of interview. The interviewer has to arrange a place to hold the interview and has to make arrangements to get there. The telephone interview requires far less resourcing. Many more people can be interviewed by telephone in the time it would take to perform just one face-to-face interview. However, telephone interviews are less personal than their face-to-face counterpart and all of the body language data will be lost using this method; they are perhaps best used for short and very focused interviews.

FIGURE 2.3 Mentoring scheme – mentor interview schedule

Research in Action
Project MR:47

MENTOR INTERVIEW SCHEDULE

Name: Title/Position:

School:

Date of interview: Interviewer:

Introduction (to be read to mentor)

As you know, I work for Research in Action and we've been asked to visit all the schools in the area that are piloting mentoring schemes. The purpose of this visit is to learn as much as possible about the experiences of providers and pupils, so that we can report to policy makers in local authorities and central government, and offer practical advice to others who will be setting up summer schools in the future.

I have a tape recorder with me. It is standard practice to record these interviews as a back up to my notes. The interview is confidential in that no individual or school will be named in the report corresponding to these interviews.

(*Unless the interviewee has any objections, tape-record the interview.*)

Are there any general questions you'd like to ask me about the research before we begin?

Your involvement

Q1: I'd like to start by asking you how you became involved in these mentoring schemes?
(*Prompt: Volunteered, nominated, persuaded?*)

Q2: In which activities are you involved?

Q3: Are you paid for your involvement?

Q4: Do you receive any other benefit for your involvement?

Your role

Q5:   What is your main role in the mentoring scheme?

Q6:   Have you got a written job description?
      (*If Yes, ask interviewee for a copy.*)

Q7:   What qualities and particular expertise do you bring to this
      kind of work?

Q8:   Did you receive any training or preparation before becoming a
      mentor?
      (*If Yes, prompt with: Who provided it? What did it entail? Was
      it helpful?*)

Evaluation

Q9:   In what ways do you think the mentoring scheme is helping to
      meet learner needs?

Q10: So far, what aspects of the mentoring programme have been
      particularly successful?

Q11: Are there any aspects of the scheme that have proved difficult
      or are not working so well?

Q12: Are there any issues with regard to involving children/young
      people with special educational needs?

Additional information

That was all I really wanted to ask you. I'll review what you have
said to me so that we can make sure that I have understood you
correctly.

(*Summarise the main points made by the interviewee.*)

Is there anything you would like to add to what you have said? Or
would you like to ask me any further questions about the research
work?

Thank you very much for your help with this research.

FIGURE 2.4 Mentoring scheme – learner interview schedule

Research in Action
Project MR:47

PUPIL INTERVIEW SCHEDULE

Name   **Year group**

School

Date of interview   **Interviewer**

Introduction (to be read to learner)

My name is _____. I work for Research in Action, and we are visiting a number of schools in the area asking people about their involvement in mentoring schemes. We want to find out as much as possible about schemes so that we can help other schools to set up their own programmes for mentoring. The questions I will be asking you have no right or wrong answers, and everything you say will be treated confidentially. No one will be named in any report that will be written, nor will I tell any teacher what you have said.

I have a tape recorder with me. It is standard practice to record these interviews as a back up to my notes.

(*Unless the interviewee has any objections, tape-record the interview.*)

Are there any general questions you'd like to ask me about the research before we begin?

(*Interviewer to use the name for the mentoring scheme in question, if it has one.*)

Q1: Before it started, what did you think a mentoring scheme was?

Q2: What kinds of things do you do with your mentor?

Q3: Are the things you and your mentor do, like the things you do at school?
(If not the same, prompt: how is it different?)

Q4: Do you think that your mentor will help you with your schoolwork?

Q5: Do you like having a mentor?

Q6: What are the best things about having a mentor?

Q7: What are the worst things about having a mentor?

Q8: How do you think the mentoring programme at your school could be improved?

Additional information

That was all I really wanted to ask you. I'll quickly read back to you what you have said so that we can make sure that I have understood you correctly.

(Summarise the main points made by the interviewee.)

Is there anything you would like to add?

Thank you very much for your help with this research.

Where a more exploratory approach is required, the face-to-face interview is to be preferred. The example set out below which, when utilised, is tailored to particular respondents (Figure 2.5) has been used for many years by the software firm Xandex Computers to anticipate demand for future products.

FIGURE 2.5 Sample telephone survey (Xandex Computers)

Xandex Computer Equipment Survey
(2003/04 data)

Date of interview

Interviewer

Interview number

Time start   (a.m./p.m.)

Time   (a.m./p.m.)

Original respondent name, title and organisation

Hello. My name is [*enter name of interviewer*], as a customer of Xandex we value your comments on the products and services we provide. This is **not** a sales call, we want to make our level of service to our best customers even better. As (*enter name of interviewee's organisation*) is one of our priority customers we would value any comments you have on some additional products and services we are thinking of introducing. This call should take no more than ten minutes of your time.

Section 1:

General Training Requirements

Question 1: Would now be a convenient time for you to answer our questions?

Yes	(*Proceed with questions.*)	1
No	(*Arrange to call back at more convenient time.*)	2
Refusal	(*Terminate call and note response.*)	3

Thank you. I'd like to start by asking you a few questions about training programmes we are currently developing.

As you will know, Xandex currently supplies all computing essentials for the modern office including state-of-the-art software and hardware. Some of this software and hardware can be difficult to use initially. We believe a day-long programme of intensive software training aimed at all staff could improve organisational performance. We can provide training for the following software packages [*insert names of software packages relevant to this organisation*].

Question 2: If this training were offered at an appropriate time, place and price would your organisation have:

a great need for this training?	1
some need for this training?	2
little or no need for this training?	3

What makes you say that? (Ask for explanation of answer given.)

Question 3: How do you currently meet your training needs in terms of acquaintance with computer software?

Section 2:

Training Requirements

We believe at Xandex that training needs differ between types of staff. Technical support staff require detailed training relating to the operating systems upon which the software is based. Management staff require focused training in relation to using the software at a high level, optimising organisational performance through its use, and identifying aspects of it worthy of delegation to others. Operations staff (such as administrators, secretaries and clerks) require detailed knowledge of the operations and functions the software is capable of performing, as well as procedures to add value to their work.

Question 4: For each staff grouping – technical, management and operations – does your organisation have:

a great need for this training?	1	
some need for this training?	2	**Technical support staff**
little or no need for this training?	3	

What makes you say that? (Ask for explanation of answer given.)

a great need for this training?	1	
some need for this training?	2	**Management staff**
little or no need for this training?	3	

What makes you say that? [Ask for explanation of answer given.]

a great need for this training?	1	**Operations staff**
some need for this training?	2	**(including**
little or no need for this training?	3	**administrators,**
		secretaries, and clerks)

What makes you say that? (Ask for explanation of answer given.)

Question 5: On a rating scale of 1 to 10 (1 being least important and 10 being most important) how important is it that your organisation invests in such training for:

	0-10 rating
technical support staff	_____
management staff	_____
operations staff	_____

Question 6: As a percentage of your annual training budget, how much would you dedicate to the training we have just outlined for:

	% of annual training budget
technical support staff	_____
management staff	_____
operations staff	_____

(*If percentage is less than 10% ask why.*)

Question 7: Would you consider Xandex an appropriate provider for the training we have talked about?

Yes	1
No	2

What makes you say that? (Ask for explanation of answer given.)

Question 8: Thank you for taking this call and answering my questions.

Because you've provided us with such useful information would you be willing to talk again to help enhance our service at Xandex?

Yes	1
No	2

Thank you very much.

END INTERVIEW

Analysing the interview data

The final stage of the interview process begins by drawing together the data collected and structuring them in such a way as to make ready for analysis. In small-scale work, this would typically involve grouping the responses to each question from all interviewees to make comparison between respondents easy (the cut-and-paste function of most wordprocessors is ideal for this). Using this approach allows themes, issues and concerns to be easily identified and quantified. When analysing a large number of interview transcripts it may be necessary to utilise the functions of computer-based tools. *NU.DIST* and *NVIVO* are two commercially available packages that facilitate interrogation and analysis of qualitative interview data. However, they rely on a coding structure that has to be developed by the researcher before any meaningful analysis can take place. (We discuss, in detail, coding and categorising qualitative – textual – data generated by interviews in Chapter 3 – Content analysis.)

We conclude this discussion by outlining the advantages and disadvantages of using interviews (Box 2.5), followed by a checklist for planning and conducting interviews (Box 2.6).

BOX 2.5 Advantages and disadvantages of using interviews

Advantages

♦ Because of your indirect involvement as a researcher, you can achieve a 100 per cent response rate for your questions.

♦ You can decide on follow-up questions (considering whether they are appropriate, or if you can glean any further useful information by asking them).

♦ You 'hear' far more than just what the participant 'tells' you. You can observe body language and interpret the tone of a response to a question.

♦ Participants often see interviews as opportunities to voice opinions and 'let off steam' about subjects.

♦ In most cases, they provide vast amounts of rich and useful data for further analysis.

Disadvantages

♦ A good interviewer requires considerable training in interview techniques.

♦ Interviews are time-consuming and costly to conduct. As a rule of thumb, you should allow two days' transcription time for one full day of interviewing.

---

continued   63

♦ Data generated through interviews can prove difficult for the lone researcher to analyse.

♦ Interpretations of interview data may differ between researchers. Whose interpretation should be applied?

♦ Unless strictly controlled, interviews can easily meander from the main subject.

BOX 2.6 Interview checklist

Interview checklist – planning and conducting the interview

♦ Have you decided what questions you will ask?

♦ How will you order the questions (will you leave contextual questions until the end of the interview)?

♦ Will the interview follow a rigid structure or will you allow some deviation from your notes?

♦ What devices will you use to record the interview (will you take notes or will you tape-record the session)?

♦ Have you piloted your interview and incorporated any useful comments or suggestions that were made?

♦ Are there any complicated or ambiguous questions (have you practised how you will explain these, or will you provide examples)?

♦ Have you identified your interview group?

♦ Is it representative?

♦ Have you arranged to meet at a suitable place (are you confident that you won't be interrupted)?

♦ Have you communicated the timing of the interview to the relevant people (obviously this includes the interviewee but may also include their work colleagues)?

♦ How will you position yourself in the interview (face-to-face or side-by-side)

♦ Have you prepared a briefing for the interview (will you read this or present it to the interviewee to read)?

♦ Can you assure anonymity to the interviewee?

♦ Have you explained how the data will be used?

♦ How will you thank the interviewee (will you offer to send feedback on the research)?

Key textbooks focusing on developing and using interviews

For those new to research

Anderson, G. (1996) 'Using interviews for successful data collection', in *Fundamentals of Educational Research*, Basingstoke: Falmer Press, pp. 222–32.

Gary Anderson's text covers a number of issues of interest to the social sciences researcher, and includes a short chapter focusing on the uses of the interview as a research technique. His clear style presents the essential points to bear in mind when considering the use of interviews within a research project. The chapter briefly summarises the types of interview, planning considerations, interviewer skills and methods of controlling the interview.

For the intermediate researcher

Gillham, B. (2000b) *The Research Interview*, London: Continuum Books, 96 pp., indexed.

This pocket-sized text provides a succinct analysis of the uses of the research interview. The book opens by exploring the nature of the interview and its use as a fundamental research tool. It presents the case for and that against using interviews, and provides a great deal of advice on framing questions, organising and managing the interview, and piloting. In addition, the text provides a useful summary of key approaches to the analysis of interview data, with a particular focus on content analysis.

For the expert

Silverman, D. (2000) *Doing Qualitative Research*, London: Sage.

This text is not aimed exclusively at 'the expert' – it is written in a very understandable and accessible way. The reason we include it here, and under this heading, is that it provides more depth and discussion of analytical techniques for exploring qualitative material (such as is generated by interviews) than do many other texts. It discusses the power of the interview as a research instrument, and goes into some detail in its consideration of a number of theoretical and practical approaches to analysis. Drawing on his own work and that of other expert qualitative researchers, David Silverman presents a text rich in approaches to collecting and analysing qualitative data – of which the application and analysis of interviews forms a crucial part.

Content analysis

What is content analysis?

In other chapters we discuss the collection of data through a number of instruments including questionnaires, interviews and focus groups. Within these instruments we have also discussed and detailed the procedures and conventions for recording responses to open-ended questions. Usually, such responses are transcribed for subsequent analysis. But what form should this analysis take? How is the content of your collected data best analysed? With closed interview or questionnaire questions it is relatively easy to begin analysis. Frequency counts, standard deviations and other statistical measures can quickly be applied and developed.

Textual data are different. How do we apply meaning to the content of responses to open-ended questions in questionnaires, interview transcripts or focus-group notes? This is essentially what content analysis does – it applies significance or meaning to information you have collected and helps to identify patterns in the text. Content analysis is an extremely broad area of research – its coverage includes both quantitative and qualitative approaches to analysis. We begin this chapter by focusing on some of the more common quantitative methods before moving on to discuss qualitative approaches to content analysis.

As a research technique, content analysis has been used in a variety of ways and within a number of contexts. It has been successfully used to analyse text and solve issues of disputed authorship of academic papers: the techniques used have included an examination of prior writings and a frequency count of nouns or commonly occurring words to help determine the probability of authorship. In the early 1990s content analysis was used to establish the identity of the 'anonymous' author of the fictional text *Primary Colors* (Foster 1996), and it has also been used, controversially, to help determine how many people actually wrote the plays attributed to Shakespeare (Mostyn 1985).

Content analysis can be used as a powerful research tool to determine, from the content of a message, sound inferences concerning the attitude of the speaker or writer. It has been usefully employed as a descriptor of diverse research techniques used for systematically collecting, analysing and making inferences from messages (North *et al.* 1963).

More recently, Krippendorff has stated content analysis to be simply 'a research technique for making replicable and valid inferences from data to their context' (1980: 21).

Often the message is delivered as a text, or converted to one (for example, an interview transcript may be produced or focus-group notes may be developed). Other examples of texts suitable for content analysis include essays, journal articles, books and chapters in books, discussions, newspaper articles or stories, speeches, conversations and advertisements. In essence content analysis is based on the assumption that an analysis of language in use can reveal meanings, priorities and understandings, and ways of organising and seeing the world.

Content analysis, which has been used as a research instrument for many years, was initially a time-consuming process. While we can now analyse varying types of datum using computer software, in the early days of content analysis much of the work was done with little automation. This often restricted analyses to simple frequency counts of identified words and terms. The introduction of ever-more sophisticated processing equipment (in the form of mainframe computers and the advancing development of personal computers) has enabled content analysis to move beyond word counts to consider such issues as the relationship between words and phrases. It is now becoming a powerful agent in the development of artificial intelligence – being used to draw conclusions and make inferences from messages.

Basic principles

Whilst the tools used for analysis may have changed and developed, the essential principles of content analysis have remained constant. To conduct a content analysis, the data (the text of an interview, speech or focus-group discussion) are coded or grouped into categories which are tested for their reliability and validity (whether or not they accurately represent what is being said, in a transcript for example). These categories or codes will include words or themes, word senses, phrases or whole sentences. Once coded, the textual data are interpreted and the results of the analysis provided. This process is shown in Box 3.1. Either of two methods is usually used: conceptual analysis and relational analysis.

BOX 3.1 Content analysis flowchart

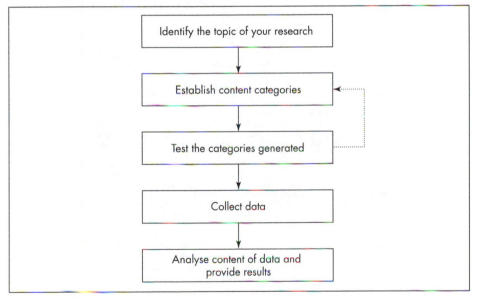

Conceptual analysis

Of the two main approaches to content analysis, conceptual analysis is by far the more popular. This approach examines either the incidence or the frequency of concepts (themes/issues, words, phrases, etc.) in a text. It quantifies the occurrences of the concepts you have chosen for examination. Conceptual analysis is also referred to as *thematic* analysis because it is the themes or issues in the text that the researcher intends to analyse.

If we consider the theme, 'police' to be of interest we could begin to analyse our documents by searching for this word. Using the article in Figure 3.1, we can determine that our theme occurs seven times (you'll see that we've simply counted the number of times this word occurs). If we broaden our concept to include the cognate words 'policing' and 'officer(s)', we can state that our theme of 'police' occurs thirteen times ('police' occurs seven times, 'policing' three times, and 'officer(s)' three times).

Police go under TV spotlight

A TWO-HOUR documentary on the work of Thames Valley Police is to be broadcast this weekend — 20 years after the first fly-on-the-wall series featuring the force caused huge controversy.

Police 2001, made by award-winning film maker Roger Graef, sets out to portray 'real' policing and features officers from Oxford, and other police areas, together with the work of some of the force's departments.

Mr Graef made a controversial documentary series about Thames Valley in 1981. This year, the BBC commissioned him to make another programme about the force.

Chief Constable Sir Charles Pollard said: "The first series was responsible for changing the way in which the police deal with rape victims and attracted a lot of attention, partly because it was one of the first fly-on-the-wall programmes about police work.

"Twenty years on Roger has returned, once again to show policing how it really is and, hopefully, once again his film will change attitudes.

"What Roger has done is to portray the predicament of policing. Most police work, if it doesn't result in an arrest, is not recorded or measured. But the reality is that every day officers are dealing with complex, difficult and sometimes thankless tasks where no crime has been committed, so officially all that work doesn't count.

"I hope the programme will improve understanding of police work and will reassure the public that we have some outstanding officers out there whose professionalism, attitude and patience is second to none."

After the original film was shown, the force came in for huge criticism. Complaints centred on a 50-minute interview of an alleged rape victim.

Police 2001 will be screened on BBC2 on Sunday at 9pm.

FIGURE 3.1 Establishing themes (*Oxford Times*, 21.11.2001)

At this level, conceptual analysis is relatively straightforward and simple. However, the themes for conceptual analysis may be *implicit* rather than explicitly stated, like those in the example discussed above. The explicit themes may include 'police', 'controversy' and 'film and television'. But what might be the implicit themes? If you were looking to establish the theme of 'workload', could you state confidently that it was present in this text? You would need to argue your case, perhaps by indicating that 'workload' is implied by the reference to police officers 'dealing with complex, difficult and sometimes thankless tasks'.

Often, content analyses are conducted on a number of text pieces in order to explore the coverage of particular themes. The theme might be crime and the use of weapons: so a useful start might be to establish the number of times words relating to weapons occur in the written pieces. Figures 3.2 and 3.3 provide extracts from articles relating to crime published in a regional newspaper. We can see that 'weapon(s)' is used three times across the pieces (none in the first article and three in the second). If we interpret this term to include also words relating to specific weapons (such as 'knife', 'blade', etc.) then the number of uses increases to eight across the pieces (five in the first article and three in the second).

In total, there are eight stages to consider in conducting an effective conceptual analysis. These are shown in Box 3.2 on page 72.

FIGURE 3.2 Exploring the use of terms relating to 'weapons' (1) (*Yorkshire Post*, 16.1.2002)

Boy slashed across face in knife attack by school bully

Kate O'Hara

A BOY has been scarred for life after being slashed across the face with a three-inch blade by a classroom bully.

Twelve-year-old Andrew Hardman now has a two-inch V-shaped cut from his eye to his nose after the attack.

Andrew, from Dewsbury, said he had been bullied ever since starting Earls Heaton High School and is now too frightened ever to go back.

He said yesterday: "It all happened quite fast and I didn't think I was actually cut, I thought he'd just struck out at me. Then my friend said I was bleeding and I realised it was quite bad. I said to the boy, 'What have you slashed me with?' and he showed me the knife. It was one of those fold-away ones."

Andrew said he was frequently the victim of bullies who would pin him down in an American wrestler-style attack. "I was already frightened at school because of the bullies. Now there's no way I'll ever go back there. It's just too dangerous."

Andrew's mother, Maria, 33, said he would remain at home until a place was found at another school.

The incident happened when a boy in Andrew's classroom started causing trouble. Andrew got out of his chair and moved towards the boy, who thought he was going to fight him, so struck out with the knife. Mrs Hardman was called at home an hour later. She said she and her husband, John, 29, a builder, were constantly going to see teachers about the bullying problem but felt it was not being dealt with.

"We have been to the school on several occasions and they just say they will talk to the bullies but it has obviously not been good enough."

Mrs Hardman said the family called police and were told by the school that the boy had been excluded for five days.

She added: "After five days he will be back at school and that is just not good enough."

Head teacher Paul Levey said yesterday: "An incident took place between two young pupils in lower school. A small knife was produced and one of the boys sustained a small cut to the cheek. One of the boys concerned has been temporarily excluded pending investigations by the school.

"The incident will be discussed by the governors at tonight's scheduled meeting. The incident will be dealt with responsibly and carefully."

Knife amnesty: Page 9.

Schools crackdown

SCHOOLS are to be told to get tough on pupils who carry weapons or repeatedly bully classmates, in a government move to respond to growing concern over violence in the classrooms.

And appeals panels are to be urged not to reinstate young-sters expelled for these reasons, but instead to send them to special units to address their anti-social behaviour, said an Education Department spokesman.

Education Secretary Estelle Morris will next week launch guidelines for schools and appeals panels on violent behaviour by pupils. For the first time, carrying a weapon will be added to the list of misdemeanours for which children can be expelled on a first offence.

And panels will be told that headteachers' decisions to perma-nently exclude persistent bullies and children carrying weapons should not normally be overruled.

FIGURE 3.3 Exploring the use of terms relating to 'weapons' (2) (*Yorkshire Post*, 16.1.2002)

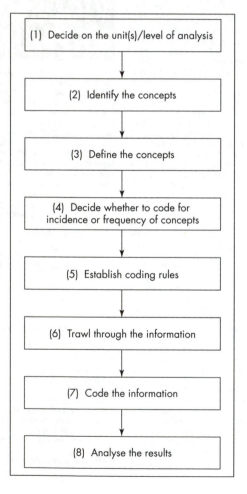

(1) Decide on the unit(s)/level of analysis

(2) Identify the concepts

(3) Define the concepts

(4) Decide whether to code for incidence or frequency of concepts

(5) Establish coding rules

(6) Trawl through the information

(7) Code the information

(8) Analyse the results

BOX 3.2 Stages in the conceptual analysis process

Before textual data are analysed, a decision has to be made concerning the unit(s)/the level of analysis. For example, are you going to code for a single word or for a set of words or phrases? In some cases, and in an attempt to provide more useful context, sentences or strings of words (such as those contained in lines of text as they appear on the page) are used as levels or units of analysis. For example, in Box 3.3 a useful and functional level of analysis would be rows or lines of text. Some computer-based text analysis packages facilitate and encourage coding in this way.

BOX 3.3 Units/levels of analysis (*Oxford Times*, 21.11.2001)

Police divers on TV

Line 1 The work of the Thames Valley Police underwater search team has been
2 the focus of a television documentary. *Divers in Blue*, which was shown
3 last week on Carlton, followed Sgt Gill Williams and her eight-strong
4 team at work. It was shot by documentary maker Mr Simon Rawles over a
5 five-day period at the end of April. Sgt Williams said: 'It was initially
6 quite strange having a camera crew literally peering over our shoulders as
7 we went about our job, but after the first day or two you tended to forget
8 they were there.' The underwater search team serves not only Thames
9 Valley Police, but also other forces.

Concepts are the issues, themes or concerns you will search for in your analysis. At the concepts stage you must develop a list of codes or categories to be used in your subsequent coding. You must decide how many concepts you will code for, which ones are the most relevant, and how much flexibility you will allow in your coding. For example, will words that do not exactly match your codes be ignored or included?

Will your coding frame allow you to include new categories as you examine the data or will your concepts be strictly pre-defined? Indicating at the outset of your research the number of categories or codes to be included will allow you to quickly analyse text and code for very specific things. However, developing new codes as you progress with your analysis provides a more flexible, rich and inclusive (and time-consuming!) analysis of the information you have collected.

DEFINING THE CONCEPTS

In this stage it is important to be specific about the concepts that are to be coded as the same issue. For example, would you code or classify 'controversial' as having the same essential meaning as 'controversially'? This stage is where you clearly define your codes (in writing) to allow you (and possibly other researchers) to consistently apply the right codes to the analysed text. Your concept definitions may provide for words with closely similar meanings to be included. In Box 3.4 we show a number of words and phrases used in a recent content analysis of interview transcripts to indicate 'a liar'.

BOX 3.4 Coding frame for the term 'liar'

Code L1   (*Instruction to coders*: include all possible permutations of tense and spelling in the identifiers below.)

liar
tells/telling porkies
fibber
economical with the truth
falsifies
untruthful
talks rubbish
unbelievable

CODING FOR INCIDENCE OR FREQUENCY?

Once the researcher has selected a number or set of concepts for coding, a decision has to be taken on whether to code for their incidence or for their frequency of occurrence – an important decision because it has implications for the coding process itself. When coding for mere incidence, 'police' in a given text would be counted once only, no matter how many times it occurs in the text. This is coding of a very basic kind, one which offers a limited perspective on the text in question. On the other hand, coding for the frequency of 'police' might give a better indication of its importance in the text. For example, thirty-five mentions of 'crime' in a text, but only two incidences of 'police' might indicate that criminal activity was predominating over the forces of law and order.

ESTABLISHING CODING RULES

Clear coding rules will allow you to 'collapse' codes into broader coding categories. For example, it might be a coding rule that 'untruthful' should be included within the 'lies' category, along with others words and phrases, such as 'is economical with the truth'. Establishing, and communicating, clear coding rules will help to prevent words being incorrectly classified. Coding rules are sometimes referred to as 'transition rules' – he or she provide, for example, that 'TV' should be classified as 'home entertainment' rather than 'watching movies', and that any subsequent occurrence of the term should be interpreted as 'home entertainment'. Applying and consistently observing such coding rules allows for comparability and maintains the validity of your data.

TRAWLING THROUGH THE INFORMATION

When you begin to trawl through or examine your data you will discover that not all of the information lends itself to coding within the codes established. You must decide what to do with this information. If it is beyond your coding frame then you may seek to amend your codes to include it. However, if the additional information adds little to your study then it may be worth considering excluding it in order to focus more on the codable content. Often words such as 'and', 'the' and 'that' can be disregarded as he or she have no impact upon the analysis.

CODING THE INFORMATION

Following development of your codes or categories, you can begin to code your text. In many instances, this can be done by hand when reading through each interview transcript, applying the codes to the information as you progress. With large numbers of interview transcripts it may be necessary to use computer-assisted coding. Many packages now available can code vast amounts of data quickly and accurately: *NU*DIST* is a very popular computer analysis package that can deal with a large amount of data and assign codes to text. However, caution must be exercised when using computerised analysis packages. It is relatively easy for you as a researcher to manually code text and identify nuances of meaning through the order of the words and the use of slang and regional variation. Computerised analysis can only do what you tell it to do: it cannot think for itself and contextualise words as a researcher might.

The last stage in any conceptual content analysis is to analyse the results of your coding. Here you would provide information as to, say, how many times the word 'health' appears compared to the occurrence of the word 'education' in a group of interview transcripts. Or you may wish to compare positive and negative comments from a number of TV news reports. You could interpret the results of your comparisons as indicative, say, of the importance of health over education, or the prevalence of negative over positive news reports.

Whilst conceptual analysis is a very useful and much-used tool, it is a *quantitative* exercise. Some argue that it fails to take account of true meanings behind information and data. To better understand the information or the text before us, we must consider the relationships between words and phrases and explore their emphases. This is what relational analysis attempts to do.

Qualitative content analysis

In essence, the stages of the content analysis process, just outlined, focus on the number of times a word, theme or issue emerges, and meaning is applied to that numerical data. Qualitative researchers argue that because some form of quantification occurs, the real meanings of the data are overlooked in favour of frequencies (Berelson 1971). Qualitative research is concerned with capturing the richness, and describing the unique complexities, of data. Some argue that counting numbers so dilutes the quality of the information collected as to make it of little use. Additionally, there are many researchers who argue that themes and issues can be determined more readily through a qualitative, more holistic, approach rather than by employing advanced statistical and analytical techniques. Reading a number of newspaper articles to establish key issues, rather than subjecting them to predefined searches for key words and phrases, allows a more thorough and accurate analysis to take place. It is often the case that themes and issues can be established quickly using a qualitative approach, rather than the more resource-intensive and time-consuming quantitative approach. The former requires no predefined coding frame to be applied; nor does it require complex numerical analysis (Mostyn 1985).

In work championing the usefulness of qualitative content analysis, it has been stated (e.g. by Berelson 1971) that quantitative content analysis should be used *only* when three factors are present: that is to say, when:

1   You are interested in very precise results.
2   There is the possibility of the collected data being biased.
3   The data collected will be statistically related to numerical data.

There are a number of techniques favoured by qualitative researchers who employ content analysis methods; one approach is to use a relational analysis model to examine content.

Relational analysis

As with other content analysis models, relational analysis begins by identifying themes or issues to explore. However, unlike the majority of other analyses, this approach attempts to explore and identify *relationships* between the themes or issues. Using this more qualitative model of analysis allows researchers to establish significant relationships between words or phrases. Relationships, rather than concepts, are the focus of this model, and individual words, phrases and themes are viewed as themselves having no inherent meaning; the meaning sought by relational analysis is established through an exploration of the links and relationships between a text's concepts, words or phrases. It might help here to think of concepts not as semantic units, packages of meaning, but rather as symbols – in some ways like those used in mathematics and logic – which acquire their meaning through their relations with other such symbols in the text. Another would be to think of concepts as units whose meaning has been replaced in each case by some other value, numerical for instance.

There are eight stages involved in the relational analysis model displayed in Box 3.5.

DECIDING ON THE QUESTION

Stating your question explicitly at the beginning of your analysis gives focus to your work. Carefully crafted research questions can limit the number of themes and issues, and their types, to be explored, making the whole process more manageable. A question, or theme, suitable for relational analysis might be what is being said in a number of newspaper articles about the cost of health care.

FRAMING THE ANALYSIS

When the question has been established, it is necessary to frame your analysis. In our health care example this might be to frame or limit the analysis sample to four or five newspaper articles dealing with issues relevant to health care.

BOX 3.5 Stages in the relational analysis process

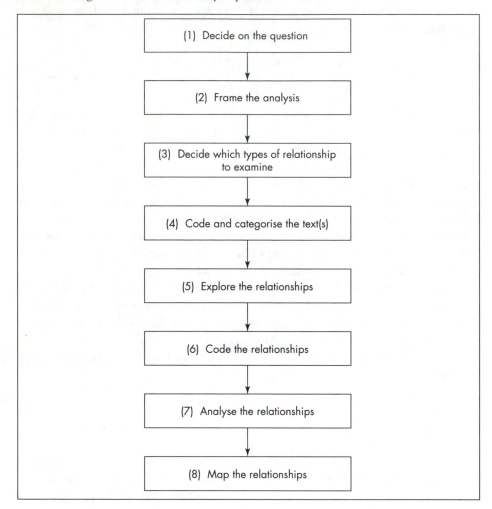

When examining relationships between words, phrases or other units of analysis, a number of approaches are possible. These include:

- affect extraction
- proximity analysis and
- cognitive mapping.

A relationship analysis based on *affect extraction* develops an emotional evaluation of themes and issues. While useful, this can be a difficult analysis to perform as emotional assessment of themes and issues can change with time and between researchers. Nevertheless, this analysis tool can usefully be employed to help determine the emotional/psychological state of a writer by exploring his or her language use.

Proximity analysis explores text for the presence of words or themes and determines their proximity to other (pre-defined) words or themes. Using this approach, the researcher would begin by defining a string of words (such as a sentence, line or paragraph of text) within which the analysis will take place. This 'window' is then scanned for the presence of the pre-defined words. Meaning is inferred from the proximity of words. Often, when proximity analysis is used, matrices and clusters of relationships are established which focus on the distance between words, and then apply weightings and meaning to those distances.

Figure 3.4 provides some sample material discussing health and health care issues. If we were examining the management of health services, we might reasonably begin by looking at words or concepts that are in close proximity to indicators of the term 'management'. For example, we might establish a relationship between management and salaries (see fifth paragraph, where 'managers' and 'pay' are mentioned), and we might additionally indicate a relationship between hospital management and hospital control (third paragraph where 'management' and 'private sector' are mentioned).

Cognitive mapping provides a *further* level of analysis once affect extraction or proximity analysis has been performed. This relational analysis technique allows researchers to generate a model of the overall meaning of the text rather than of specific elements within it. Often cognitive mapping techniques result in a graphical representation of the linkages between words or concepts to provide a network of the relationships that exist (Carley 1990).

FIGURE 3.4 Examining the management of health services (*Yorkshire Post*, 16.1.2002)

Milburn forced on defensive over NHS future

HEALTH Secretary Alan Milburn last night was forced to defend plans to allow private companies to run failing hospitals after they came under fierce attack from unions and his own party.

Mr Milburn's announcement that England's poorest hospitals could be franchised came as a French hospital prepared to receive the first NHS patients to be sent abroad for treatment.

The radical plans would allow the private sector, charities and universities to take over the management of the poorest-performing hospitals.

Unions immediately attacked the move as a recipe for chaos and warned it could lead to some hospitals poaching desperately-needed staff from elsewhere in the NHS.

Dave Prentis, general secretary of Unison, said pay problems which blighted the railways could spread to the NHS if different rates of pay were set by managers brought in from the private sector.

Wakefield MP David Hinchliffe, Labour chairman of the influential health select committee, attacked Mr Milburn's vision as "incredibly worrying".

CODING AND CATEGORISE THE TEXT

The decision about the type of analysis to perform will inform decisions about which words or concepts to code and categorise. In our health care example, it might be decided to code for positive and negative comments made about the cost of health care. In this case, the researcher would scan the text(s) and classify words/comments as positive and negative.

EXPLORING RELATIONSHIPS

A number of tools are available in the relational analysis model that allow researchers to explore linkages and relationships between words or concepts. The strength of a relationship can be displayed by examining words or concepts and establishing (given their location in the text, number of times used, association with the central theme or themes of the research, etc.) the clarity of the connections that may exist. It is often useful to display strength relationships in numerical form, ranging from 0 (no relationship) to +1 (direct relationship).

Another means of exploring relationships is to establish whether words of concepts are related at all. Often, using this exploratory tool, researchers determine the extent to which words or concepts are positively or negatively related. By way of a simple example, in research work exploring 'health care provision in the UK', the term 'cost' could have a negative association, whereas 'health' could have a positive one. Using this tool to signify a relationship allows researchers to develop complex linkages, based on strength associations between words or concepts.

CODING THE RELATIONSHIPS

This stage of analysis provides the main difference between conceptual analysis and relational analysis. While conceptual analysis focuses on the words or concepts, in relational analysis the focus is on the relationships between words or concepts. Therefore the relationships themselves are coded under this analysis. Many codes and relationship permutations are possible – such as codes indicating weighting, codes indicating positive relationships and codes indicating negative relationships.

Analysis of your coded information using a relational approach can involve extremely complex statistical techniques. For example, you can examine all your heavily weighted codes and seek to establish linkages between positive and negative words or concepts. Additionally, you may explore linkages to search for directional relationships. Does the existence of a coded word or phrase have an impact on subsequent coding? Does your coding suggest the existence of other factors or influences?

Relational analysis allows a graphical representation of relationships. This is often useful when analysing your data and presenting it to others. You can quickly establish the strengths and weaknesses of relationships, including positive and negative attributes, visually.

Different approaches to content analysis

In this chapter we have looked at two very different approaches to content analysis. The first approach, using a conceptual analysis model, is essentially quantitative – categories are developed and coded, and the number of occurrences of themes or issues is recorded. This is a very popular method with researchers new to content analysis and who are accustomed to analysing data in the more traditional, numerical way. We provide an example from research of our own using conceptual analysis in Figure 3.5 on page 82.

The relational analysis approach to content analysis detailed in this chapter can be said to focus momre upon the meaning of what is being said (Berelson 1971). A number of researchers (Berelson 1971; Krippendorff 1980) believe an approach based on relationships is a more accurate way to interpet the content of textual material. We believe that both the conceptual and the relational approaches are valid tools for analysing what is being said in any communication, whether in newspaper articles, journals, speeches, etc. You must decide, given your research topic and your approach to research itself, which of the two broad approaches to employ. As an example, and using the material provided in Figures 3.6–3.10, utilise one of the two methods we have detailed to analyse the newspaper articles on health issues. Ask a colleague to do the same and compare your notes. Do you use the same approach? If yes, why is this? Do you develop similar or the same categories or themes? Are your results similar? How do/can you justify your results?

FIGURE 3.5 Content analysis of the social sciences

CONTENT ANALYSIS IN ACTION

In a recent study, we examined the reporting of the social sciences in the British mass media. A central theme was to categorise what was being said, or written, about social science research in the UK. Sources consulted over a year-long period included: twelve national newspapers, four local newspapers, a number of magazines, national and local television news programmes, and national and local radio news programmes (Fenton *et al.* 1998: 40). All sources were scanned for mentions of research conducted by social science researchers, and codes were subsequently developed.

The data collected indicated that coverage of social science research was wide-ranging and covered a number of themes and issues, as displayed in the table below. The analysis also allowed the research team to begin to develop an understanding of why some issues are reported in the media more than others, as well as providing valuable insights into who are judged by journalists to be influential and authoritative figures in social science research.

Coverage of social science research[a]

Theme/topic	% of sources reporting on research
Social integration and control	40
Children	6
Crime	5
Education	7
Work/employment/unemployment	5
Race/ethnic minorities	3
Sexual behaviour	3
Gender	5
UK economy	17
Private sector producers	3
Health	11
Moods/mental states	7
Lifestyles and relationships	10
Relationships	6
UK government politics and policy	9
Public policy impact	5
Social analysis – general	6
Organisations/small business	4
Demographics	5
Foreign economies and international trade	1

[a] *Source*: Fenton *et al.* 1998: 34

FIGURE 3.6 'Health' issues (1) (*Oxford Times*, 21.11.2001)

920 inquiries outstanding

Families face wait for news on organs

By Victoria Owen

ALMOST 1,000 bereaved families will have to wait more than a year to discover if Oxford doctors kept their relatives' brains.

NHS managers at the John Radcliffe Hospital had 1,700 inquiries after revealing that 4,400 organs had been retained after patients' deaths.

Now they have admitted that many people will not receive an answer until next year.

The organ retention team had hoped to contact all the families concerned by Christmas.

Although 720 enquires have been answered and many organs have been returned to relatives, staff have another 920 families left to contact.

Ms Julie Hartley-Jones, Oxford Radcliffe Hospitals NHS Trust chief nurse, said: "We thought that we would get this work done by Christmas.

"It's quite clear that we're not going to be able to get to that stage and we have a number of families to get back to.

"We will postpone everything on December 7, because we don't want families to be sent information at the same time as they are getting Christmas cards. But we will write to

families to let them know we are temporarily stopping."

Many of the remaining queries relate to patients from as far back as the 1940s, that need further investigation because they are linked to other hospitals.

Bereaved mother Mrs Linda Frampton, of Ascott-under-Wychwood, is still to hear whether her stillborn daughter Katie was one of hundreds of babies whose brains were removed.

Mrs Frampton said: "I think it's appalling that we're going to have to wait even longer. There must be so much suffering, because I'm not the only person affected. It's just too much for people to cope with."

It was revealed in January that Oxford pathologists had kept organs for neurological research.

Hospital managers immediately set up a special helpline and carried out an in-depth search of 15,000 rooms at the John Radcliffe, Churchill and Radcliffe Infirmary, Oxford, and The Horton, Banbury, to make sure no tissue samples had been left uncatalogued.

They then had to wait until being given the all-clear to release information to relatives.

Treatment could save thousands of lives

TENS of thousands of lives could be saved each year if people suffering heart problems took cholesterol-lowering drugs, according to top Oxford University academics.

A seven-year study led by Prof Rory Collins, at the university's clinical trial service unit, has found a third of all heart attacks and strokes in people with cardiovascular trouble could be avoided if they took drugs known as statins.

Prof Collins said: "This is a stunning result with massive public health implications.

"We've found that cholesterol-lowering treatment can protect a far wider range of people than was previously thought."

The £21m Heart Protection Study, funded by the Medical Research Council, the British Heart Foundation, and pharmaceutical companies Merck & Co. Inc and Roche Vitamins, involved 20,000 volunteers, aged 40-80, who were at high risk of coronary heart disease.

Prof Collins said: "In this trial 10,000 people were on a statin. If now an extra ten million high-risk people worldwide go on to statin treatment, this would save about 50,000 lives each year — that's a thousand a week.

"These results are at least as important as previous findings for aspirin's effects on heart attack and strokes.

"Those findings changed medical practice, and we expect these to have the same effect."

FIGURE 3.7 'Health' issues (2)

New baby blood test pioneered at the JR

A TEST to monitor unborn babies by using their mothers' blood which was developed in Oxford is set to be used worldwide.

The procedure, designed by blood specialists at the John Radcliffe Hospital, Oxford, is due to be used in the United States, Australia, Europe and Japan.

By using blood from the mother, the test pinpoints whether a baby has any serious genetic defects.

It can also identify the child's blood group, and in the future it may replace more uncomfortable tests.

Consultant haematologist, Prof Jim Wainscoat, led a team to develop the new blood test. The research began in 1988.

They found that, in samples from expectant mothers, plasma, an ingredient of blood, contained genetic material from their unborn babies.

Prof Wainscoat said: "I think it has got a lot of potential. At first it sounded strange that the plasma material which people threw down the sink turns out to be the most interesting part of the blood.

"Five years ago there was a sense of shock. It seems normal now."

The test has the potential to replace a number of procedures which are uncomfortable for mothers, as well as dangerous to babies.

One is amniocentesis, where a needle is used to take samples of fluid surrounding the baby to look for signs of Down's Syndrome.

Prof Wainscoat said: "In the future we shall see it as strange to take a mother's blood to look at not only how the mother is doing, but also how the baby is doing.

"I would hope that in the future invasive treatment techniques for prenatal diagnosis can be avoided."

The blood test has been developed jointly by Oxford Radcliffe Hospitals NHS Trust research and development department, and Oxford University.

It is now being licensed for use in Asia and the Pacific, Europe, and the USA.

FIGURE 3.8 'Health' issues (3)

FIGURE 3.9 'Health' issues (4)

Hospital project's opponents give up their fight

OPPONENTS to a hospital and housing development on Oxford United's former ground have given up their fight.

At the first meeting of Oxford City Council's north east area committee, at Wood Farm First School, in Titup Hall Drive, Headington, councillors voted not to challenge a planning inquiry's decision to allow the development to go ahead.

The Acland Hospital, part of the independent Nuffield Hospital Group, plans to build a state-of-the-art hospital at the Manor Ground in Headington.

The scheme also includes plans by property developer Bellway Homes for 90 flats.

Oxford City Council objected to the development on the grounds that it would increase traffic congestion in Headington. There were also concerns that the proposed hospital building would be overbearing for properties in Horwood Close.

Mr Paul Semple, from Oxford City Council's community services department, described the appeal decision as "exceptionally regrettable", but told the meeting that the council's legal department advised there were no grounds to overturn it through the High Court.

Hospitals to spend £200,000 on signs

HOSPITAL managers are to spend £200,000 on new ideas to prevent visitors getting lost.

The "wayfinding" scheme could transform sculptures and artwork into landmarks to help orientate people walking around the John Radcliffe, Churchill and Radcliffe Infirmary, Oxford, and The Horton Hospital, Banbury.

New signs will also be designed so they can be used by the visually impaired and the disabled.

Mr Ian Humphries, estates director for the Oxford Radcliffe Hospitals NHS Trust, said a lot of work had been done to assist people travelling around the buildings, but signage was "generally poor and inconsistent".

He said: "We do get complaints and we get a lot of people lost and confused and wandering around the sites.

"What we need to get around our sites is a consistent system — not one that has built up over a number of years."

The wayfinding scheme will include road signs for easy access to the hospitals, as well as "you are here" maps and a colour-coding system to mark out specific departments, buildings and areas of each hospital.

Trust transport manager Mr David Edwards, who is leading the project, said signage would be colour contrasting to make it easy for visually impaired people to see.

He said: "We have to ensure that it is all low enough for visually-impaired people to see and it could also be tactile so you can feel the shape.

"We may also use Braille on lift buttons, but not all around the hospital, although it is something we've considered in the eye hospital at the Radcliffe Infirmary."

The scheme is due to take three years to complete.

FIGURE 3.10 'Health' issues (5)

Key textbooks focusing on developing and using content analysis

For those new to research

> Edwards, A. and Talbot, R. (1994) *The Hard-Pressed Researcher: A Research Handbook for the Caring Professions*, London: Longman.

This is a general book covering research methods for those in the caring professions. Chapter 5 discusses a variety of appropriate methods for collecting and analysing data, and is in part dedicated to content analysis. Pages 102–110 provide an accessible description of content analysis for those new to the subject. Useful information is provided on developing meaningful categories and devising appropriate coding frames. The section closes with a comment on the uses of quantitative and qualitative models.

For the intermediate researcher

> Weber, R.P. (1990) *Basic Content Analysis*, 2nd edition, London: Sage.

This text provides an interesting and readable introduction to the subject of content analysis. Each chapter is well written in an accessible style. The book begins with an overview of content analysis, followed, in Chapter 2, by a detailed discussion of classification methods, leading to the development and creation of coding schemes and categories. A number of approaches to content analysis are covered in the book, with information provided on particular strengths and limitations. As with most texts on the subject, this one is aimed at academics, students and professionals across the social sciences.

For the expert

> Krippendorff, K. (1980) *Content Analysis: An Introduction to its Methodology*, Beverly Hills, CA: Sage.

This comprehensive text is widely used and quoted, despite being more than twenty years' old. Klaus Krippendorff begins by discussing the history of content analysis, before moving on to cover its conceptual foundations. In its fourteen chapters, the book details a number of models of analysis and incorporates material on the validity and reliability of data. Consideration is also given to computerised analysis of data, although some of the approaches outlined may appear outdated due to advances in computer-assisted data analysis. In many parts of the text, Krippendorff compares content analysis to other techniques and provides evidence of what it can and can not do.

Focus groups

There can be few people who emerge from a particularly uncomfortable job interview feeling that they had said everything they wanted to say, and in the way they wanted to say it, to the panel sitting opposite them. With the eyes of all the interviewers on you, and their attending to your every word, the pressure to do your best can seem overwhelming. You are on your own. The panel has prepared in advance the questions you will be asked. You are expected to answer whatever is put to you. The panel's members have some idea of what counts as a good or a bad answer to each of those questions. They are judging your performance, which has as much to do with your temperament, your preparation and your attitude as the relevant professional knowledge, skills and experiences you could bring to the job. You are in competition with the other interviewees and your answers will be compared with theirs, yet you may never set eyes on them yourself and you may never know their responses to the same questions.

Luckily, not all interview situations are as daunting as job interviews. Thankfully, there are other types. One-to-one research interviews, for example, whether structured, semi-structured or unstructured, are a popular, non-threatening and highly useful research instrument, as Chapter 2 testifies. While such interviews may contain some of the features of the job interview – for example, a series of prepared questions to be asked of a number of people individually – those features are adapted and modified to suit the purposes of the research exercise.

What are focus-group interviews?

Focus-group interviews are at the opposite end of the spectrum altogether, modified yet further until they resemble hardly at all the kinds of interviews you are obliged to endure in your efforts to find your ideal job. Focus-group research is a form of qualitative method used to gather rich, descriptive data in a small-group format from participants who have agreed to 'focus' on a topic of mutual interest. The emphasis is on understanding participants' experiences, interests, attitudes, perspectives and assumptions. Our favourite definition of the focus-group interview – one which captures all of its essential characteristics – is provided by Anderson:

> A focus group is a carefully planned and moderated informal discussion where one person's ideas bounce off another's creating a chain reaction of informative dialogue. Its purpose is to address a specific topic, in depth, in a comfortable environment to elicit a wide range of opinions, attitudes, feelings or perceptions from a group of individuals who share some common experience relative to the dimension under study. The product of a focus group is a unique form of qualitative information which brings understanding about how people react to an experience or product.
>
> (Anderson 1996: 200)

Focus-group interviews have enjoyed consistent popularity over many years as an effective and economical instrument of data collection. If you have an interest in market research you will no doubt be aware of the dominance of the focus group within that field, having been utilised for decades to evaluate consumers' opinions of products and services ranging from new cars to washing powders, television programmes to customer help-lines (Greenbaum 1998). The information they produce has been used to develop better products and to encourage consumers to use or buy them. This original commercial focus has gradually widened to include consumers of education, health and community programmes and services, such as the extent of parents' support for new school facilities, patients' levels of satisfaction with their treatment at their local hospital, pensioners' thoughts on the quality of their local civic amenities, and so on. Political parties are the latest in a long line of clients of focus-group consultancies, keen to gather public opinion of their prospective parliamentary candidates and MPs, and what they stand for, with a view to maximising their appeal (Diamond and Bates 1992).

During the 1980s market researchers were joined in their use of focus groups by social science researchers. They realised that the ways in which focus group interviews are organised – in particular the relaxed and convivial setting, the unrestricted nature of the discussion, and the neutrality of the moderator – meant they were particularly suited to collecting data on sensitive, delicate and otherwise complex or difficult social issues. Research on domestic violence, mental health and sexual behaviour (particularly in relation to HIV/AIDS and contraception), for example, has increasingly utilised focus groups in the data-collection phase (Richter *et al.* 1991; Lupton and Tulloch 1996). The priorities here, however, have been to promote awareness, educate or protect vulnerable individuals and alter attitudes rather than to collect opinion.

Now, more than ever, researchers are using focus-group interviews in the data-collection phase of their projects. Whatever your own specialism or particular interest – be it education, nursing, health science, business, politics or something more unusual such as linguistics, anthropology, media studies, town-planning, sustainable development or information technology – you can be sure to find research reports in your field which feature focus-group interviews somewhere.

What is distinctive about focus groups?

Obviously, in a one-to-one interview interaction occurs between the interviewer and the interviewee. Even when a group of candidates is interviewed at the same time in the same room, perhaps for a single job, by and large interviewees tend to interact with the interviewer only and not with their fellow interviewees, and each takes his or her turn to talk. Focus-group interviews are organised along altogether different lines. Not only do they permit exactly the kind of interaction which would be inappropriate in other interview situations, but they positively encourage it. Focus groups rely for their success on the ways in which groups of people naturally engage in conversations. For example, all participants have equal access to the discussion; there are no restrictions on who may speak, how often and for how long; participants do not have to wait for their turn to speak or be given permission; and, when they do speak, what they say is not specified in advance.

Why should this kind of interaction be encouraged? It is generally agreed that individuals have their own thoughts, feelings or opinions about a certain issue which are either 'brought to the table' or formed and developed during a discussion. As at least one aim of your research project is to gain access to those opinions, then it is also generally accepted that a relatively informal meeting, with an atmosphere conducive to self-expression, held between people who share common interests and overseen by a non-judgemental moderator, provides a most effective research tool.

It is within such a situation that participants may recall details of their own experiences, release their own inhibitions and feel comfortable about contributing their own comments, and responding to comments made by other members of the group in supportive or critical ways. Consequently, the intention is that the discussion will be richer, deeper and more honest and incisive than any interview with a single participant could produce. Hess (1968: 194) summarises the benefits from the participant interactions which focus-group interviews encourage as the five 'S's, shown in Box 4.1.

BOX 4.1 The five 'S's of group interaction

- ♦ synergism
- ♦ snowballing
- ♦ stimulation
- ♦ security
- ♦ spontaneity

Synergism is a cumulative process in which individual participants react to, and build upon, the responses of other group members. The resulting combined group effort may produce a wider range of information, insight and ideas than that likely to be revealed by any single member of the group in a one-to-one interview. *Snowballing* is a situation in which a comment by one participant triggers a chain of responses from others which in turn generates new ideas and topics for discussion. *Stimulation* is a situation in which the group setting works to spur members on to express their own ideas. The *security* of a focus group interview encourages group members to express their opinions more freely, especially if they find he or she share similar opinions, or if the group members are relatively shy or lacking in confidence. The *spontaneity* of a focus-group interview refers to the fact that no individual is obliged to have a particular view or opinion about a topic and to express that view to the rest of the group, so when a participant chooses to speak in a focus-group interview it is likely to be because he or she holds a strong opinion about a subject, or agrees or disagrees emphatically with another's comments. This is in contrast to one-to-one interviews where there is a certain pressure on the interviewee to answer all questions whether or not he or she is able to provide a truthful or considered answer. The intended consequence of the spontaneity effect is data which are more heartfelt, honest and meaningful than those obtained through individual interviews. The more instances of these effects you can point to, the greater the confidence you should have that your focus-group interviews will be a success.

Krueger argues that a major strength of the focus-group interview is that it is a 'socially-oriented research procedure'. This is in contrast to other research instruments, such as mail or telephone surveys and individual interviews, which he criticises for their in-built assumption that people are perfectly able to form opinions about a topic or issue independently of one another. Krueger maintains that it is natural for people to listen to others' opinions in forming their own: 'People are social creatures who interact with others. They are influenced by the comments of others and make decisions after listening to the advice and counsel of people around them' (Krueger 2000: 34).

In a sense, the focus-group interview's 'socially oriented' approach mimics people's everyday interaction, the main advantage being that the data it yields may more accurately reflect people's genuine thoughts and feelings about a subject than that obtained through individual interviews in which respondents feel forced to answer with, perhaps, insufficient time to consider all the issues. Of course, there are those less desirable features of everyday interaction which you would want to minimise, for example the undue influence of dominant group members and individuals' reluctance to be a lone voice within a group, and we address these issues in more depth towards the end of the chapter, where we contemplate some of the disadvantages of focus groups.

Might your research benefit from conducting focus groups?

You should consider using focus groups in your research if you can answer 'Yes' to any of the questions (adapted from Wilkinson 1998) which follow.

Is it the intention of your research to explore the issue(s) under question from your subjects' own perspectives?

Researchers have many different, sometimes competing, points of view as to the purposes of carrying out research, and what the relationship between the research, the researcher and their subjects should be. One view is that the purpose of research is to understand the issue(s) under question from the standpoint of those who it most affects or to whom it most matters. This involves grounding the research in your participants' understandings of the topic as opposed to your own, no matter how closely you feel them to be aligned. Focus groups can be particularly helpful in this. They can provide the means to ensure that both your own research question(s) and the data you collect reflect the personal experiences or interests of people who care deeply about, or have been affected in some way by, your research topic.

Within your area of interest, have you yet to decide on the precise question(s) your research will seek to address?

In the earliest stages of your research you may have only a vague idea of the topic you intend to research more fully. (See how some researchers have dealt with this dilemma in Chapter 6 of this book.) By exploring different options with your group and honing in on those which dominate the discussion, a focus-group meeting may help you to define more concretely your research question(s).

During your research, do you intend to develop a questionnaire and/or a set of interview questions? Are you unsure about what questions to ask and how to ask them?

Although focus groups themselves are often used as a means of conducting research, there is no reason why they cannot be used as one of a range of data-collection methods within a larger research project. As we mention in the Introduction, we believe such a multi-method approach can be preferable to utilising a single research instrument. If your intention is to ask your research subjects a series of precise, systematically-formulated, questions about your area of interest, either in person or in the form of a questionnaire, then conducting a focus-group discussion beforehand may prove useful. It should help you to identify the kinds of questions which provoke the greatest responses, as well as help to construct your questions in such a way that respondents fully understand what you mean by them. It should also help you to weed out the weakest questions at an early stage, as well as discard questions which turn out to have been based on your own misplaced assumptions about and misunderstandings of the real issues.

Has this worked well in practice? In a recent edition of the journal *Academic Medicine* we found an essay written by three senior physicians from McGill University in Montreal reporting their positive experience of using focus groups for exactly this purpose (McLeod *et al.* 2000). They wanted to explore by means of a questionnaire the views of senior faculty members about their clinical skills, the pace of new technology and medical information, and the impact these were having on their teaching and research. In order to ensure the questionnaire would be valid and useful they held focus groups to test their own hypotheses about the major issues. While some hypotheses proved correct, others proved to be inaccurate. These findings informed the final design of the questionnaire. The exercise was so successful that we have reproduced the essay in Figure 4.1. We hope you will find it to be of help as you consider designing your own research questions.

While analysing the responses to your research questionnaires and/or interview questions has anything particularly caught your attention?

In contrast to the previous scenario, in which a focus group might be conducted prior to the development of a questionnaire and/or interview schedule to help inform its design, a focus-group discussion held in a final follow-up phase may equally benefit your research. It can provide you with an opportunity to pursue any responses to your original questions which you did not expect, or which you found exciting or thought-provoking, enabling you to add vibrancy and depth to what can often appear to be dry and uninspiring data. We have done this in our own research: we were recently involved in evaluating a local education authority's proposed changes to their rules for allocating secondary-school places. The evaluation consisted, first, of a large-scale survey addressed to parents, then a series of focus-groups, recruited from these same parents, to discuss the most passionately felt issues. We discuss this project in more depth below (pp. 99–102).

Why not also look beyond your own research? You could use a focus group to explore the findings of other researchers' survey-based findings, often to vindicate and build upon the earlier work; occasionally to test, scrutinise or cast doubt upon it.

ESSAY

Using Focus Groups to Design a Valid Questionnaire

Peter J. McLeod, MD, Tim W. Meagher, MB, Yvonne Steinert, PhD, and Don Boudreau, MD

ABSTRACT

The authors planned to study the roles and concerns of senior faculty members at their institutions. To elaborate the aims of their study and to help them design a valid questionnaire, they conducted focus groups with senior faculty. The authors describe how the information gleaned from the focus groups helped them develop their questionnaire.
Acad. Med. 2000;75:671.

Faculty leaders regularly address issues important to junior faculty members, but the former generally pay little attention to their senior members.[1] Interested in researching this overlooked area, we decided to develop a questionnaire to gather information from senior physicians about their particular concerns and interests. We hypothesized that senior faculty would be concerned about such issues as keeping current with medical information and new technologies, and they they would find particularly satisfying their roles as mentors and their problem-solving abilities. To elaborate the aims of our study and to help us design a valid and useful questionnaire, we decided to conduct focus groups.

To begin, each of us independently developed questions designed to elicit the concerns and experiences of older faculty members; each list was circulated to all authors for comment. After several iterations we found that the

questions could roughly be categorized into the four classic domains of a medical school: research, teaching, practice, and administration. For each domain, three to four open-ended "trigger questions" evolved. For example, one trigger question in the teaching domain was "How have your teaching skills evolved as you have matured?"

Next, we recruited a sample of senior academic physicians 50 or older to participate in one of two focus groups. The first group consisted of four physicians whose career emphasis was clinical practice and teaching; the second group was composed of three physicians with research-oriented careers. One of the authors (PJM) and a research assistant met with each group for two hours. Using the list of trigger questions, we encouraged the participants to share ideas and concerns about achieving senior status and to talk about their own experiences and their suggestions for others reaching senior status. We audiotaped and transcribed each session for content-analysis purposes.

All group members' concerns fit the four academic domains, although their individual emphases varied. We learned that some of our hypotheses were on the mark and others were not. For example, contrary to our initial assumptions, all of the senior faculty felt comfortable with their clinical practice skills, and found that new technology in the clinical or research domains presented no threat, since technicians and junior colleagues with technical expertise were readily available. As we suspected, they perceived their clinical

judgement and problem-solving skills to be at their peak.

We used the focus-group data to develop a questionnaire based on the four career domains. We then sent the questionnaire to a convenience sample of ten senior academic physicians to assess its readability and comprehensibility; this led to some further modifications. The final version of the questionnaire was three pages long, with seven parts of ten questions each.

We predict that the information we acquire from a faculty-wide survey of senior academic physicians can be used to address the real concerns of senior faculty, to guide administrators, and to formulate practical advice for faculty approaching senior status. Our results suggest that focus groups can be helpful in facilitating the development of useful and valid research questionnaires.

Dr. McLeod *is professor of medicine and pharmacology, McGill University (MU);* **Dr. Meagher** *is associate physician-in-chief, MU Health Centre;* **Dr. Steinert** *is associate professor, family medicine, MU; and* **Dr. Boudreau** *is associate dean for undergraduate education, MU; all in Montreal, Quebec, Canada.*

Address correspondence and requests for reprints to Dr. McLeod, Department of Medicine, The Montreal General Hospital, 1650 Cedar Avenue, Montreal, Quebec H3G 1A4, Canada; e-mail: ⟨peter.mcleod@muhc.mcgill.ca⟩.

REFERENCE

1. Mathis CB. Academic Careers and Adult Development: A Nexus for Research—Current Issues in Higher Education. No. 2. Faculty Career Development. Washington, DC: American Association for Higher Education, 1979: 21–4.

FIGURE 4.1 A positive experience of using focus groups

Are you conducting your research with the aim of actively changing, rather than simply describing or exploring, a situation?

Focus groups have occasionally been used to empower citizens and to foster social change, rather than only to identify and describe the social situations which might benefit from it. Research which utilises focus groups in this way tends to be overtly politically motivated. The purpose of the research is to isolate participants' problems, dissatisfactions or other negative experiences, understand them thoroughly and bring about solutions. In other words, your purpose might be to provide a voice for those who otherwise would not be heard. Examples include focus-group research to identify how Hispanic students may overcome barriers to success in American schools (Padilla 1983) and research to provide practicable means to ease the plight of women subjected to domestic violence (Mies 1983).

BOX 4.2 Summary of the purposes of a focus-group interview

- ♦ To gather insight to, or raise awareness of, an issue or topic
- ♦ To uncover complex motivations, attitudes or behaviours
- ♦ To prepare for a larger study
- ♦ To interpret previously obtained research results
- ♦ To develop new research questions and issues for further exploration
- ♦ To obtain market research data
- ♦ To develop understanding of consumers
- ♦ To stimulate new ideas and creative concepts
- ♦ To discern participants' needs when planning, improving or evaluating services
- ♦ To identify problems with existing services
- ♦ To learn how respondents talk in their own words about your focus of interest

---

Conducting focus-group interviews

There are many things to consider in the planning stages of your focus-group interviews. These include: who should participate in your focus groups; how you should approach them; what kinds of questions you should ask, and how many; how the focus groups should be conducted; where to hold the focus groups; and how to collect and analyse your data. Here we guide you through the process, step-by-step (Box 4.3), taking these considerations in turn and drawing on our own experiences of conducting focus groups to point you in the right direction.

BOX 4.3 Stages in conducting focus-group research

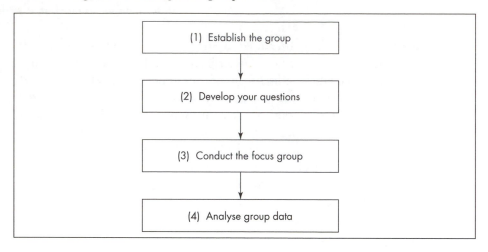

Step 1: Establishing your focus group

The group is made up of participants. It need not contain a fixed number of participants (though fewer than four may jeopardise the valuable group dynamic you seek, and more than twelve may make the group unwieldy); nor does there need to be a fixed number of groups in your research project (though if you have only one you risk observing the dynamics of that group and little else), nor a fixed number of meetings to be held with your group. The most productive focus group discussions are invariably those in which the participants have strong opinions most likely from personal experience about the topic or issue you are researching. This can become the glue which bonds the group together.

You may choose a group which pre-exists your research exercise, for example teachers at a given school, medical staff on a particular ward, or supervisors on one factory floor. Some researchers have expressed reservations about picking such 'intact' groups, arguing that individual participants may feel obliged to make only comments of which their friends and colleagues would approve. It is more common to collect together participants who are strangers to one another but share similar qualities, perhaps in terms of educational qualifications, age range, occupation, political affiliation, ethnic origin, sexual orientation or medical condition. Occasionally, you may want your participants to be representative of the 'general public' or the 'person on the street'. We ourselves have conducted focus groups for which the topic under discussion was the general public's perception of newspaper articles, television programmes and other media items which reported social science in some way (Fenton *et al.* 1998: Chapter 6). To manage the exercise, we divided our sample of the general public into small focus groups according to sex (men and women), highest educational qualification (GCSE, A Level, higher education) and employment (public sector, private sector). In doing so, we were aiming to explore whether individuals' social and cultural experiences influenced their views of social science reports.

To ensure the make-up of your group meets your criteria you will need to screen your potential participants to ensure they possess the characteristics you require. Screening produces a 'sampling frame'. This is simply a whittled-down sample of people selected from every possible category of suitable participant, and it is from that sampling frame that you should recruit your focus groups. Screening is usually conducted via telephone, email or letter of invitation, and consists of a brief summary of your research project, a short list of questions designed to identify appropriate focus-group members, and of course a request for their co-operation should they meet your criteria. To illustrate what we mean by a screening process we provide two examples from our own experience.

Screening process examples

NEW ARRANGEMENTS FOR ALLOCATING SCHOOL PLACES

A research project with which we were involved attempted to gauge parents' opinions of their local education authority's proposed changes to the way in which pupils were allocated a secondary-school place. As you might imagine, this proved to be a very emotive subject. The vast majority of parents cared very deeply about which secondary school their children would attend, especially if they considered their child would be disadvantaged by the proposed system for allocating places. We had first researched parents' views using a questionnaire, sent to 4,000 homes. The recipients comprised potential participants of focus-group interviews designed to supplement and enrich the questionnaire data. By asking, at the end of the questionnaire, whether recipients would be interested in taking part in further group discussions we were able to generate a sampling frame made up of those who agreed. On that basis, we were able to select from our sampling frame discrete focus groups according to specific criteria such as geographical location, degree of satisfaction with the proposed arrangements, the source of their information, social or medical factors relating to their own children, and so on.

NEW TECHNOLOGY TO TEACH HISTORY

We have reproduced in Figure 4.2 a real letter of invitation we developed during a recent research project exploring cutting-edge interactive multimedia software for the study of history in secondary schools. A local software company had developed the basic prototype of a virtual medieval village which pupils could 'visit' on screen. They could explore the manor house, a feudal farm and peasant dwellings, investigate their design and construction, and, over the course of a single day from dawn until dusk observe and interact with the village's inhabitants. The developers wanted to ensure their program was educationally sound, so we thought it would be helpful to arrange for the programmers and a number of enthusiastic practising history teachers to get together. (Please feel free to use the letter as a template for a similar letter of invitation in your own research.)

In this example, our potential participants were heads of history departments in local secondary schools, although as you can see from the letter we had no objection to expanding the population by encouraging recipients to pass on the invitation to other interested history teachers. This letter was sent to twenty heads of department with the expectation that not everyone would be able or willing to attend. Those who responded positively – ten in all – became our sampling frame. The focus group went ahead with two software designers and five teachers who we chose because they were happy to trial the prototype software in their schools.

Step 2: Developing your questions

Your participants should feel he or she are taking part in a free-flowing discussion, exploring a variety of related issues and covering a range of topics on their own terms and in their own time, rather than being exposed to a series of probing questions. Nevertheless, you will have to take the time to construct your questions carefully, so that they can be embedded neatly, and non-threateningly, in your group discussion when the time comes. You should need far fewer questions than you would develop for one-to-one interviews as in a focus-group situation each question can lead to a substantial amount of discussion and debate. We recommend that you begin with a brainstorming session in which you write down as many questions as seem pertinent, beginning, if appropriate, with the question(s) which acted as the impetus for your research. Next, reduce and refine them by asking yourself 'which of these questions are the most important and which will my possible participants be able to answer?', until you are left with half-a-dozen or so crucial questions. Consider the wording of your questions. Encourage as much talk about your research focus as possible by ensuring that all your questions are open-ended (see Chapters 1 and 2 to find out what this means, and Box 4.4 for other advice on questioning technique). Lastly, order them in a way which ensures a natural flow from one to the next.

In the research project concerned with proposed changes to rules for allocating school places, we developed a set of five questions for our focus-group

To all history colleagues

The medieval village: ICT in history discussion group

We write to you about some very exciting work currently in progress regarding the use of ICT in history. This work focuses on high-level software to support the study of the unit Medieval Realms: Britain 1066–1500 at Key Stage 3 of the National Curriculum for history. This project aims to combine the expertise of teachers and software developers to produce software which will add an extra dimension to the ways in which history teachers already work with their classes.

We are now at a stage of development at which teachers can play an active and influential role in helping to create software that will be of real practical use in the classroom. In the first instance, we are contacting heads of history in a number of local schools simply to invite you, along with any other interested colleagues, to come along to the Department of Educational Studies to take part in an informal discussion about the best ways forward.

We intend to demonstrate the software in its current form, in order (a) to capture teachers' initial reactions, first impressions, comments and suggestions, and (b) to prompt a brainstorming session surrounding how the software might be refined in order to incorporate teachers' requirements and wishes.

We hope to hold the meeting between 4.30 and 6.00 p.m. on Monday, 3 April. Should you be willing to come along to our first meeting and take part in our research we would be very grateful if you could let us know as soon as possible by telephoning us directly on (xxxxx) xxxxxx, or by fax on (xxxxx) xxxxxx. Alternatively, we can be contacted at our email address: xxxxxxxxxxxxxxxxxxx

We would like to assure you that our involvement in this project is entirely for educational reasons. We have no commercial interest in this development.

Refreshments will be provided and your travel expenses will be covered. We very much look forward to hearing from you.

With best wishes

Peter Birmingham
Research Officer

FIGURE 4.2 Example invitation to take part in a focus group

BOX 4.4   Good questioning

- ◆ Begin with general and positive questions which are easy to answer in order to engage and reassure your participants
- ◆ Move on to specific key questions which focus on your issue of concern and may be more challenging
- ◆ Use probing or follow-up questions in light of participants' comments. Try to get to the heart of the matter
- ◆ Ensure that your questions make sense and are respectfully expressed. Do they get the kind of response you want?
- ◆ Test out your questions with colleagues or friends, and revise them where necessary

interviews based on the more impassioned responses from our original questionnaire to parents. Our focus-group questions included:

- • Which children should be given priority in allocations of school places?
- • How did parents feel about the information pack they had received from the county council?
- • How helpful had the county council been in responding to parents' questions and concerns?
- • How did parents feel about the school which had offered their child a place? and
- • How could the current system be improved?

You may wish to develop a detailed script for your focus group (as in Box 4.5), of which your questions will form the central section. The process of writing a script helps you to put your questions in context for the participants. A script also helps to ensure that each focus-group interview is conducted in a similar fashion, making the results more reliable and helping the moderator to stay on track and on time.

To illustrate the kind of thing we mean by 'opening section' we have reproduced in Figure 4.3 the opening remarks to the focus-group interview held for the Medieval Village research project.

BOX 4.5 The three sections of a focus group script

1   *The opening section* covers the facilitator's welcoming of the group; the purpose and context of the focus group are introduced, what a focus group is and how it will flow are explained, and the introductions are made.
2   *The question section* is where you ask the questions you have developed.
3   *The closing section* is for thanking the participants, giving them an opportunity for further input, telling them how the data will be used, and explaining when the larger process will be completed.

Step 3: Conducting your focus group

It is likely that you, alone or together with one or more friends, colleagues or co-researchers, will act as moderator during the focus-group meeting. It is the responsibility of the moderator to ensure the meeting is a successful one – by organising a seating plan for the participants in as comfortable and convivial a setting as possible, welcoming them to the discussion and putting them at their ease, allowing each participant the time to introduce himself or herself to the rest of the group and to make comments when they wish, ensuring that all participants can make eye contact with one another as well as hear each other, arranging for the discussion to be recorded (on audio-tape or mini-disk, or even video), outlining the purpose of the meeting to the group, and so on. Your single most important responsibility as moderator is to ask the research questions, but to do so by introducing them appropriately, probing further, pausing to let participants have their say, involving all participants and always remaining neutral and impartial towards the comments your participants offer (see Box 4.6).

Despite the potential for discussions to go 'off the rails' due to the flexible and non-prescriptive way in which they are organised, the skilled moderator will not allow the group to lose sight of the designated topic. One way to achieve this is by means of the stimuli which often accompany research questions. Stimuli may take the form of documents, short reports, press cuttings, segments of television programmes, new packaging for an ageing product, cards to sort into a preferred order, some kind of game to play, a flip-chart on which are summarised key moments of the discussion, and so on. It may be that you would like the group to talk about these stimuli in their own right, or that you would like the stimuli to 'spark off' a discussion about some related matter. The focus group in the Medieval Village project featured only one stimulus – the computer program itself, which was demonstrated to the group by the software's designers at the start of the

Moderator: What we've got here is the creation of an environment that operates on real physics and in real time. You can actually wander around this village in the morning and meet a certain set of characters, and you can come back a couple of hours later or towards the end of the day and meet other characters in those spots, or the same characters having different conversations. The shadows will all change and there will be different seasons. As far as this meeting is concerned, as we explained in the letter, we really want to pick your brains and tap into your expertise, and as I see things going we want to introduce you to the Medieval Village and get your feelings on it. From there we want you to think about where we can take this work and what we can do with it. And then we'd like to explore what this means in terms of your classrooms and how this fits in with the context you're working in. But before all that, let's begin with some introductions.

CT: My name is CT. I'm head of history at . . . and I'm interested in when, and when not, is the best time to use ICT.

MD: I'm MD and I teach history and ICT at . . . I think it's quite interesting to use ICT to teach the subject.

JI: My name's JI. I have an average capability myself, and have started to use ICT increasingly this year but I find we haven't got very good equipment at. . . . It's very difficult to get on the network, and when you get there it crashes. Also my department's a problem. You can't convince them that they can do things with ICT that they can't do with scissors and glue.

DG: I'm DG and I work at. . . . We got criticised in 1997 by Ofsted for being no good at ICT. We're still no good at ICT, and they're coming back next year, so we ought to try and do something about it. We hardly use it at all except for wordprocessing. That's pretty much the limit for most of our students at the moment.

IG: My name is IG and I'm head of history at. . . . I have just taken over the department and I'm currently revamping what we do with ICT at Key Stage 3. We're a technology college, so we have access to two networked rooms and students are encouraged to use ICT at every single possible opportunity. Within the department it's principally used for wordprocessing.

FIGURE 4.3 Opening section of the Medieval Village focus group interview

BOX 4.6 Tips for the focus-group moderator

- Be comfortable with group processes
- Encourage discussion
- Balance the contributions
- Listen
- Paraphrase and summarise participants' comments

- Be empathetic and sensitive
- Function as a facilitator, not a performer
- Keep the discussion moving and focused
- Use silences, pauses and probes effectively
- Exert mild control, but avoid leading the participants

- Remain flexible and adaptive
- Stay in the background – it is the opinions of the participants that are wanted
- Suspend your personal biases
- Acknowledge individual contributions
- Remain conscious of time

- Be respectful to the participants and thank them for their contributions
- Have adequate background knowledge of the topic
- Have effective communication skills
- Understand how to use humour and naïve questions
- Thank participants for their time and contribution

(Adapted from Anderson 1998: 204)

meeting, and intermittently throughout, to stimulate and encourage the discussion. In the case of the public's perceptions of social science project we used eight separate stimuli, including broadsheet press cuttings, popular magazine articles, radio programme extracts and segments from television news bulletins, turning to each in turn to prompt discussion and debate.

The purpose of the focus-group interview is not to achieve consensus among participants but to identify and explore all the issues surrounding your research question until the perspectives have been exhausted. With this in mind, a skilled moderator will build up the momentum of the meeting and encourage the participants to be enthusiastic contributors to the discussion. Techniques to achieve this include addressing individuals directly by name ('Why do you feel that way, Neil?' 'Emma, what do you feel about what Clare said?'), drawing out participants by asking broad questions ('There are a couple of people we haven't heard from yet. Eric, do you have an opinion? Ann, do you have a perspective on this?'), verifying, restating or paraphrasing what you have heard ('So what I think you're saying, David, is . . .'), probing further when participants simply express agreement or disagreement with another's comments ('Kelvin, I noticed you nod then. Why was that?') Additionally, do not underestimate the power of silence. Pauses in the conversation can be uncomfortable enough for some people to feel obliged to resume speaking or begin talking in response to someone else's comments.

Although you should always arrange to record each interview, either on audio-tape, mini-disc or on video, we recommend that you also take detailed notes throughout each session in case the technology lets you down. We know from our own experience how dispiriting it can be for a researcher to oversee discussions which are full of incisive debate and argument related to the research topic, only to discover that the tape-recorder had broken for some unknown reason half-way through, and then to realise that the notes taken at the time were totally inadequate and full of holes. Paying full attention to the discussion and taking notes at the same time takes a long time to master. For that reason we recommend you divide the two tasks between yourself and a colleague. Your notes should include verbatim accounts of the views of individual participants which particularly illustrate the sentiments of the group, the names of the individuals contributing those comments and the strength of feeling with which comments were made. You should also try to note down facial expressions, nods of agreement or disagreement and other gestures which are impossible to capture in an audio-recording, again referring to who made them, when, and in response to what. You should also jot down in the margin of your notes the approximate time when each of these things occurred so that you can locate them on the tape later. It is never a waste of your time to make detailed notes, even if your tape-recorder works perfectly on every occasion. Your notes will serve to contribute to the next task – data analysis – by enriching and enhancing the information you have captured in your recordings.

Step 4: Analysing your data

There is no avoiding the first task involved in analysing your data – transcribing your tapes in order to produce an accurate record of everything which was said in each of your focus-group interviews. This may appear a daunting and unappealing chore. After all, you may be conducting a whole series of discussions, each lasting an hour or more. In order to make the prospect slightly more palatable, we recommend that you transcribe each recording as soon as possible after each meeting, when participants' comments are still fresh in your mind. There are few sights a researcher finds more unpleasant than a backlog of interview recordings, going back weeks or months, in need of transcribing. When you do transcribe your data, you may find the job easier by tidying it up as you go. Exclude any coughs, sneezes, hesitations, false starts, trip-ups and repetitions you hear, and feel free to correct speakers' use of grammar as long as the meaning of their comments remains intact. Include with each transcript other documents and any accompanying information you may have collected from each interview, such as copies of flip-chart entries, your own handwritten notes and those of your participants, and any stimuli used in the session. Compile everything and produce a preliminary record of each session, noting any big ideas, important themes or concepts which you feel arose from the discussion.

Once you have completed a preliminary record of all of your focus-group interviews, your next task is to scrutinise, carefully and closely, the content of your data. Begin your content analysis by reading all your summaries and transcripts in one sitting. During this phase the themes and ideas you have identified in your preliminary analysis become a starting point for organising and categorising your data in terms of the themes, patterns and trends which encompass *all* of your discussions and not any single discussion in isolation. Consider the language used by your participants, as well as the context, frequency and intensity of their comments and the extent to which they held on to or changed their opinions and viewpoints. Look for the unexpected, the counter-intuitive comment which surprises you. These may illuminate your own research prejudices or assumptions about the issue you are exploring, as well as reveal the thoughts and feelings of your group members.

As you explore your data the categories you develop will act as a framework for understanding and working with the information you have collected. We recommend that you distinguish between the themes, patterns and issues by colour-coding your categories. This can be achieved very simply by hand, using highlighter pens on printed transcripts or different fonts and font colours alongside the cut-and-paste facility in your wordprocessor. (Further tips are given in Box 4.7.) Increasingly, specialised software for the analysis of qualitative data is being adopted by researchers. Computer programs such as *The Ethnograph*, *NU*DIST* and *ATLAS.ti* can search for key phrases and the frequency with which certain words are used and in what context. They can also compare categories, test out new categories and link them together in ways which allow researchers to explore their data in great depth and detail. For a closer look at the use of computer software for analysing qualitative data we recommend you consult Seale (2000) or Kelle (1995), and Catterall and Maclaran (1997) in relation to focus-group data in particular. Chapter 3 of this book offers an introduction to content analysis.

BOX 4.7 Tips for analysing your data

♦ Transcribe your interviews
♦ Type up significant notes
♦ Gather together transcripts, notes and other documents in a preliminary record
♦ Cut-and-paste your data into themes, patterns, trends, etc., whether manually, with your wordprocessor or with specialised analysis software
♦ Organise your categories into subcategories and arrange them in order of importance
♦ Edit your data to remove any extraneous details and to ensure you reflect your interviews in a fair, balanced and accurate way
♦ Select and edit actual quotations to illustrate your emerging themes, taking care to avoid extreme views and to ensure participants' identities are concealed
♦ Think about investigating emerging issues further, perhaps by using alternative instruments

---

Disadvantages of focus groups

Ironically, the greatest strength of focus groups – their group dynamics and interactions – can also be the source of their greatest weakness. It would be remiss of us not to make you aware of the two most frequently cited limitations of focus group research.

Inference within and beyond the group

The unit of analysis in the focus group is *the group*. This means that findings which emerge from a focus-group interview are not equal to the opinions or ideas of any individual member; nor are they capable of being inferred to any population beyond the group. Neither is it possible to discern with confidence the opinions of each member in the focus group because every statement he or she makes might have been influenced by the interaction of the group as a whole in the following ways and to an unknowable degree.

First, participants may respond in ways designed to please others. If participants join the focus group in pursuit of a reward, they may be more conscious of pleasing a moderator or a sponsor than of contributing honestly and truthfully to the discussion. Alternatively, an individual member may have a particular reason to please someone else in the group. Second, individual group members are, by and large, unwilling to diverge too far from the group consensus. On the whole, people are reluctant to contradict prevailing viewpoints. Third, participants may choose not to reveal certain information in a group setting – especially that which is complicated, highly personal or sensitive – and, in concealing such information, data which may have proven invaluable for your own research would remain hidden from view. Fourth, the 'leader effect' of dominant individuals is a frequently observed phenomenon. Members may be influenced by opinions of the leader who best articulates their opinions. Although the moderator can try to prevent the leader from monopolising the interview, it is difficult to analyse the extent to which he or she has influenced the opinions of others. Furthermore, group dynamics sometimes generate 'hot-housing' or 'polarisation' effects by which emotions in already heated discussions escalate out of all proportion.

Working with a group

The selection of group members is likely to affect the outcome of discussions. Demographic factors such as age, sex and occupation undoubtedly influence the character of any group. However, it is not very easy to predict the influence on a group of each individual at the recruitment stage. If individual members already know each other they may feel reluctant to speak frankly to one another. On the other hand, if members are total strangers they may be reluctant to speak because of the somewhat false and artificial environment in which they find themselves. Second, the moderator has less control over the focus group than he or she would have over one-to-one interviews. There is a trade-off operating here. The promise of animated, honest, enlivened and enriched debate and argument about an issue or topic at the heart of your research interests is offset by the risk of generating a convoluted and unfocused muddle. For that reason it may be wise to conduct several focus groups over the course of a single research project.

Nevertheless, if the purpose of your research is to gain an insight to a particular theme or issue, focus-group interviews provide a relatively natural, relaxed and secure setting in which participants are encouraged to share both positive and negative comments. The group setting allows both your own questions and your respondents' answers to be clarified and modified over the course of the interview, which in turn can enhance the group discussion and assist the chain reaction of participant dialogue. From a practical standpoint, focus-group interviews are relatively inexpensive, data-rich and versatile. You should be able to utilise them in a variety of ways and for a wide range of purposes, depending on your own particular research interests.

JI: History's about asking the right sort of questions, but it's also about being able to sift and select from information, so it is a valid way of proceeding.

IG: I think it has to be very tightly focused in the fact that my Year 7 could get quite excited by this and just wander around without actually coming to any particular conclusions, so I would have thought that to have quite focused tasks with specific questions that they could ask would be very beneficial.

MD: We tend to organise our history along various strands so that we're all working towards the task, be it an essay on something or a project on something. But what would be the skill they'd be learning?

Moderator: I think there are a range of skills, but we have the ability to tie in other things, so you can go into the church, for example, and you might overhear a conversation about the recent murder of Thomas Becket, and then go into another part of the program and find out what was going on in terms of relationships with the king. So there are lots of ways in which we can cover lots of the material which is currently within traditional textbook-type approaches to teaching the Medieval Village.

JI: If it's all spoken, I can't see it operating in a networked room, for instance, where everyone's talking at once.

MD: We've got one pair of headphones per two kids. They wouldn't be able to use this unless we suddenly get thirty computers in a room!

IG: I can see a way that, perhaps, if it was linked to things like the murder of Thomas Becket, this program can cover the whole of Medieval Realms, so you can choose times when you would want to go in and interview particular individuals. If there was an explicit link you could say 'This covers that particular aspect of the National Curriculum'. That would be extremely useful.

MD: Yeah, because you might do a three- or four-week study of the Medieval Village, but we couldn't get three or four weeks in the computer room. Usually, in the computer room, we have one lesson a year, or a term, or whatever we happen to have fought for that particular time! Not every class will get it, or you might miss it, or you might get two lessons if you're really lucky, and I couldn't guarantee this year or the year after that we would be able to get three or four lessons to do . . . and I think you'd need that.

IG: Which is why you'd need that tight focus.

JI: Or use it as just one resource within the classroom.

Moderator: As a stand-alone type of thing?

JI: Yes.

Moderator: Is one of the problems, perhaps, why as history teachers we don't use ICT so much because the quality of the programs doesn't really enable you to do what you want to do as teachers?

MD: Yes.

CT: CD ROMs, yes. I think they're appalling.

IG: Anything that is interactive is good, and there's just nothing there.

Moderator: What we're up against is that when pupils go home and they start playing Play Station games, and whatever else, they are involved in decisions like that. The graphics are much better. Does anyone have an opinion on that?

JI: A thing that worries me is the amount of information that they may get, and if they have a text transcript of the dialogue, they're then going to have to sift through all that as well. And the recording of what they find out is an issue.

Moderator: In my head that's not the case. I think you then get into reading and literacy at the moment with textbooks. My idea was that you would wander around and use this camera to capture a picture and the sound that goes with it. So, in terms of answering a question about what life was like in a medieval village, how could that be done?

IG: Is it possible, then, that you could have a task and in some form of *PowerPoint* presentation you could put together and link together? Link evidence from the clips with some statements taken from peasants, or whatever? That would be an interesting way to present it.

MD: You'd need a simpler version of that if you couldn't get the extra computer time to do it.

IG: You could do it with a stand-alone and a projector.

MD: But we don't have one for history.

IG: If it's quite clear that 'This is the task; these are the people you need to speak to; these are the sorts of questions you need to ask; and this is how you're going to present your results', whether it's a *PowerPoint* thing, whether it's an essay with a writing frame, or however you're going to do it.

Moderator: And within that, if we had various options – you could go and investigate Beckett, you could go and investigate the Peasants' Revolt, you could go and investigate the War of the Roses, whatever that thing is – if we've then got different types of activities associated with those various packages, then would that make it attractive?

MD: You probably wouldn't need to write the whole thing out. I mean we end up totally rewriting resources anyway, but you just need a general idea – you could do a PowerPoint, you could do

> this, you could do that, here's an example of something or
> other.
> *Moderator*: You see, we can actually give you more control over this
> program in terms of you deciding. How would you respond to that?
> Would you like to have an input into what's there?
> *MD*: Oh yeah!
> *IG*: I think, if you're looking at an overriding view of the feudal
> system, you'd get two kids to look at one aspect, another two
> kids another aspect. So, if you're talking about the problems of
> time within one lesson, you could perhaps get a group of kids
> that prepare something.
> *Software designer*: One thing I didn't actually mention was that the
> way it's been built is that the actual talking part of it and the
> elements that go into conversations between characters, or
> between characters and you, we're actually calling them *tableaux*.
> You can plug new ones in so we can evolve the village and add more
> information as time goes on. We could do something like a
> manorial court where you could probably study certain aspects of
> the feudal system, and you could have a large body of the village
> in there and you could witness, or even take part, I suppose, in
> the court and in the judgments of the lord or whatever.
> *Moderator*: You can actually be there at the scene of a punishment.
> *MD*: Throw your own stone, as it were!

FIGURE 4.4 Transcript extract from the Medieval Village project focus group

A practice exercise

Take a close look at the transcript we have reproduced in Figure 4.4. It is an extract from our Medieval Village focus-group interview. This book is about researching in the real world, and the transcript gives an impression of how messy that can be. As you will already have seen (Chapter 2), participants can often wander off the point or fail to provide the kinds of answers to your questions you would perhaps have expected. Nevertheless, try to identify some of the emerging themes and issues. Once you have done this, try to arrange them in order of importance, and pick out statements which most effectively illustrate the issues you have identified.

Key texts on focus-group research

For those new to research

Morgan, D.L. (1998) *The Focus Group Guidebook*, London: Sage.

This book is a user-friendly general introduction to conducting focus groups. David Morgan discusses reasons for using focus groups and what they can be used to accomplish. Intended to reassure and help those new to focus groups, this guide is all you will need to get your focus-group project underway.

For the intermediate researcher

Krueger, R.A. (2000) *Focus Groups: A Practical Guide for Applied Research*, 3rd edition, London: Sage.

This comprehensive text offers a step-by-step approach to focus-group research, and includes discussions on analysing results, developing questioning strategies, the role of the moderator, selecting participants, and accounting for cultural diversity within focus groups. This book is packed with real-life hands-on examples of focus group research.

For the expert

Wilkinson, S. (1998) 'Focus group methodology: a review', *International Journal of Social Research Methodology*, 1(3): 181–203.

This article reviews the use of focus groups across the social sciences, critically focusing on three central features of focus-group research: access to participants' own language, concepts and concerns; encouraging more fully articulated accounts; and collective sense-making in action. The article concludes with a discussion of issues in the analysis of focus-group data.

Chapter 5

Observation

In this chapter we

Picture this: You want to know how to drive a car or to score a penalty in a game of football. You have never done either of these things yourself so in order to find out how these things are done, and what it is like to do them, you decide to ask people who are adept at one or the other a series of questions, either in person in the form of a short interview or on paper by means of a quick questionnaire. What is the very first thing I should do with the car/football? Where should I place my feet and my hands? Where should I be looking? How do I stop myself from stalling the car or from kicking the football wide of the goal? How should I deal with oncoming traffic? How might I fool the goalkeeper into diving the wrong way? How can I differentiate between good and bad drivers or more and less skilful penalty-takers? These are all questions which it may be useful to ask. Your ultimate aim is to produce an instruction manual of sorts based on the answers to your questions which you (and anyone else for that matter) can then read and follow. Even though you may never have sat in the driver's seat or held a football before, all you would have to do is to follow the instructions or read thoroughly and repeatedly the descriptions you have compiled of what driving cars or scoring penalties is all about, and you would be immediately expert at either.

Somehow, we do not think we have convinced you. We think you would find this scenario a little ridiculous, not least because all the questionnaire or interview responses in the world about how these things are done would be no substitute for simply experiencing them. No matter how detailed the instructions or how meticulous the description of successful car-driving or penalty-taking, the only way to understand truly what is involved in these activities – what they mean to the people who do them, what they are 'all about' – is to watch as they are done, to see them from their perspective, to share the activities with others who are competent, possibly to try them out yourself, to practise, slowly but surely to hone your skills, to make silly errors this time but to get it right next time, and so on.

What is observation?

Merely asking about or reporting the activities people carry out in different social settings and situations will no doubt give you a flavour of what is involved, but in order to understand fully what these activities mean to people, how they themselves perceive them and what their perspective is on them, it is necessary to see those people in action, to experience what it is they do, even to wade in and have a go yourself. This is the research method called *observation*, and one of the clearest basic definitions we have found of observation as a research method tells us that it is 'research characterised by a prolonged period of intense social interaction between the researcher and the subjects, in the milieu of the latter, during which time data, in the form of field notes, are unobtrusively and systematically collected' (Bogdan 1972: 3). We refer to social scientific research of this kind throughout this chapter as 'observation', although we make no real distinction between observation and 'ethnography' – literally 'writing about people'. You may come across the term ethnography frequently. It describes essentially the same practice but one which has its roots more in anthropology than in social science.

Why choose observation?

Social researchers are interested in people and, in particular, the ways in which people act in, interpret and understand the complex world around them, whether that is the world of the classroom, the hospital, the factory floor, the head office, the local government department or wherever. How people see and understand their surroundings will no doubt play a part in the ways in which they behave, they act and interact with others, and in the ways their actions are perceived by others. Observation is an extremely handy tool for researchers in this regard. It can allow researchers to understand much more about what goes on in complex real-world situations than they can ever discover simply by asking questions of those who experience them (no matter how probing the questions may be), and by looking only at what is said about them in questionnaires and interviews. This may be because interviewees and questionnaire respondents are sometimes reluctant to impart everything they know, perhaps feeling it would be improper or insensitive to do so, or because they consider some things to be insignificant or irrelevant. It is more likely the case, however, that they are *unable* to provide information about certain events or activities, if asked outright, because they occur so regularly or appear so unremarkable and mundane that they are hardly aware of them at all.

More than just looking?

Despite the term's connotations, there is much more to observation than just looking. Of course looking is at the heart of all observation, but the best observational researchers are skilled in a technique of looking in a focused and systematic way. In fact, observation involves a range of skills, of which observing is just one. Others include listening, participating, contributing, pursuing, questioning, communicating, interacting, sharing, refraining, retreating, negotiating, timing, recording, describing, and so on. If you plan to conduct observational studies you should be prepared to engage in some or all of these activities, sometimes simultaneously, which can be at best challenging and at worst exhausting. Any thoughts you might have had that, when it comes to choosing your research instrument, observation is the easy option, dispense with them now! The observation process can be more demanding and taxing than any other research method. The settings you find yourself in, and the activities, events and interactions going on in them, may be hectic, unpredictable and confusing. Unlike that of the 'interviewer', for example, the exact role of the 'observer' is not easy to pin down, as you may find yourself adopting an assortment of smaller roles – questioner, contributor, negotiator, note-taker, and so on – within any single observation session. And once your session is underway where do the boundaries lie? What exactly do you observe and what do you ignore? It is relatively easy to begin and end interviews, but when and how do you start and stop observing and, once started, how long should you observe for?

All this may make observation seem a daunting – even frightening – prospect for the novice and the expert researcher alike, but it need not be so. With a little careful preparation observational studies can be some of the most rewarding and enjoyable research experiences you are likely to have. Before you embark on your observations, however, the very first thing to do is to decide whether this research instrument is for you; whether your approach to research and to the problem, issue or question you are interested in exploring are suited to observational research methods.

Should you consider using observation in your research?

Whatever the research project you have in mind, an observational strategy might improve it if you can answer 'Yes' to any of the questions that follow Box 5.1.

BOX 5.1 When to use observation in your research

◆   When the ways in which people behave and interact with one another in a social setting are important to your research.
◆   When you are interested in researching social settings and what happens in them.
◆   When the best way to research what you want to know is to experience it for yourself.
◆   When the context of the events you are researching is important.
◆   As a useful supplement to other research instruments.
◆   When a flexible approach to research is needed.

Do you consider the ways in which people behave and interact in a social setting to be important to your research?

Perhaps your interest lies in researching groups of people in order to understand and explore their behaviour, their actions and activities, as well as to understand how they themselves interpret and view the actions and activities of people around them; in other words, to get to grips with what it is these people do, how they get on with things, and what being a part of the group is all about. We may be talking about groups with an exclusive and relatively fixed membership, such as all the employees of a local firm, the nursing staff of one particular ward at your local hospital, a parent–teacher association meeting held at a nearby community centre, or a band of social scientists presenting papers at a prestigious annual conference. Alternatively, we might simply be talking about Saturday afternoon shoppers in the high street of your nearest town, demonstrators rallying through your neighbourhood, holidaymakers hanging around at the airport, students killing time at the local pub or coffee shop, football fans gathering at the ground before a big match, or other more amorphous groups with no fixed membership. A particularly effective way to study such groups in depth is to become part of them, immerse yourself in them, go where they go as they go there, and watch what they do as they do it. Slowly, you will be able to build up a picture of the group – a more complete and rounded picture than you would be able to construct by questioning any individual member.

Are you interested in researching social settings and what happens in them?

Perhaps your primary research interest lies less with people's group behaviour and more with the settings themselves in which people conduct their affairs: classrooms and staffrooms, courtrooms and police stations, bars and clubs, shops and offices, music festivals and student demonstrations, hospital clinics and doctors' surgeries, boardrooms and council chambers. The list is endless. The occupants may change but the settings stay the same, and time spent in them – a year, month, week, day or even an hour – has the potential to yield a rich abundance of observational data capable of illuminating the diverse roles each setting plays in our complex society. Whatever the setting, it is likely that a great deal will happen in a short space of time, most of which you would normally miss through no fault of your own. Observational studies can provide a permanent record of fleeting and transient situations, which you can use at a later date, perhaps to discover how frequently certain events occur, to compare how the same settings are used at different times of the day or how different settings are used to conduct similar activities.

Is the best way to research what you want to know to experience it for yourself?

Getting actively involved in some way in the setting you intend to research rather than standing on the sidelines can be an appealing prospect for any researcher. By means of observational studies, you can collect data about people's actions, interactions and decisions in context and at the time and location in which they occur. You will as a result know more about your research topic because you have experienced it, participated in it, shared the experience with the very people you are researching and seen all from their point of view. Compare this with the data generated via questionnaires and interviews: they may be based upon your research subjects' recollections and accounts of past events, which may be hazy and inaccurate. In interview situations, you may similarly have to rely on your subjects' ability to reconstruct and verbalize, out of context, a version of events for you. There are groups of people for whom this can be very problematic – young children, who are often shy and nervous; patients in hospital perhaps too ill to take part directly in research; and adults with learning difficulties are three such groups with whom interviews may yield very weak data. You stand to learn much more about such groups by observing them than you would by trying to interview your subjects directly.

Is the context important in which the events you are researching occur?

Questionnaire surveys and interviews are often administered after the events which form their subject matter have taken place. Additionally, some research projects, for example certain psychological tests, take place in a laboratory setting and resemble an 'experiment' in which people's behaviour is explored under controlled or artificial conditions. Such studies are sometimes criticised by observational researchers for down-playing or ignoring altogether individuals' feelings about the event, topic or issue under investigation as it would have been experienced *naturally*. In contrast to researchers working under laboratory conditions or asking about past events, those employing observational and descriptive methods in their research (see 'Capturing what you see' later in this chapter) feel the *context* in which events occur to be all-important, and are wary of the potential shortcomings of decontextualising events. So they invest time and effort in recording their data in ways which try to retain the real-life depth, richness and roundedness of the original events as they were actually experienced by their research subjects.

Will you have the opportunity to use a variety of data-collection methods in your research?

You may wish to use observation as one of several methods to explore your research questions. It is especially common for a researcher keen to conduct observational studies also to incorporate interviews with key participants in her or his research. In this way data relating to events they observe can be combined with explanations or accounts of them provided by the people most directly involved. This may happen quite spontaneously and informally in response to events as they unfold in front of the researcher and the research subjects, or it could happen in a more formal and planned way as an intentional element of the data-collection phase of a research project. Your observations may be used as the basis of your interview questions; or, vice versa, your questions may dictate what it is you should observe. There is no need to worry about which to do first: if you are unsure of your interview questions, conduct some observations to help inform them; if you are unsure of what to observe, use the answers to your interview questions to help you. Sometimes you will find a discrepancy between what you are told is the case in an interview and what you witness for yourself during an observation session, so allow yourself some freedom to tailor and adapt existing questions or to write altogether new questions in light of what you see going on around you; and remember to build in some time in which to ask them.

Can you be flexible in your approach to your research?

You may be operating under constraints of time, money and resources and, although observation can consume large amounts of all these things, it need not do. Even one hour spent observing a social setting can provide a wealth of data. Observation is also perhaps the most versatile and adaptable of all research techniques. Your research focus can change significantly and unexpectedly in response to what is happening in the situation around you – not automatically a bad thing – but you should still be able to carry on without your research being compromised. It is not as though you would have to leave the setting and develop a completely new set of interview questions or construct a totally new questionnaire. Imagine how many questions you would have to prepare in order to be confident of dealing with any unforeseen situation which might confront you as you carry out your research! Additionally, observational studies can be used to address an extensive variety of research questions, including: what is going on here? how often does this happen? how do these people interact with each other? what is it that makes this happen? why does this happen in this way? what are these people actually doing and is it what they tell me they're doing? and many more.

Planning and conducting your observation

Before embarking on the planning stages of your observation you will find it helpful to be reasonably confident of two things: *the focus of your study*, i.e. the topic of your research, what it is you wish to explore and learn more about; and *the research questions you intend to address*. Of course, both your research focus and your research questions may change over the course of your inquiries in light of your experiences. Although they may well be provisional in the beginning they are still vital. Without them you will struggle to provide some initial shape and structure to your research. It is only when you are reasonably sure of the purpose of your study and of the questions to which you seek answers that you will be able to begin thinking about the array of issues associated with observational research. These include what you will observe, how to gain access and how you will observe it, how you will conduct yourself, how you will record what you see, what additional information you will collect, and how you will process and analyse your data. We hope that by addressing each element of the observation process in a clear and structured way we will help you to feel confident enough to try observation for yourself in your own research projects.

Choosing what to observe: the social situation

One of the most difficult decisions you will have to make concerns exactly *what* will comprise the social situation(s) which will be the observational focus of your research. This will inevitably (and obviously) come down to what it is that you intend to research. All social situations possess three components: a location; the people (sometimes called actors); and the activity or activities taking place. One example of a social situation might be a consultation (activity) between a doctor and a patient (actors) held in the local surgery (location). A contrasting example would be a confrontation (activity) between striking workers, management and police (actors) at a picket line (location); and a third, the use of a new computer program (activity) by a class of pupils and their teacher (actors) in their school's ICT suite (location).

You will appreciate that there is a very real potential for social situations to be unwieldy, unmanageable and sprawling, with any number of people doing all sorts of things in all kinds of places, and with unpredictable outcomes. We believe it is always better to do modest research well than ambitious research badly, and for that reason we strongly recommend you take measures to make the enterprise a manageable one. The best way to do this is to take advantage of the activity–actor–location character of social situations and use it to frame your research. It is a question of priorities. Let us take the first example from above to show what we mean.

THE DOCTOR–PATIENT CONSULTATION

This is the activity you will research. You may be interested in

- how consultations are done or what happens during them;
- what kinds of notes the doctor takes;
- how the doctor uses the specialised medical equipment at his or her disposal;
- how long consultations take and what kinds of outcomes they have;
- how consultations at one surgery compare with those at another, and so on.

THE DOCTOR AND THE PATIENT

These are the actors you will study. You may wish to explore

- the doctor's composure and manner during consultations;
- the attitudes and behaviour of patients towards their doctor;
- how doctor and patients communicate, and with what degree of success;
- similarities and differences in the attitudes, approaches and actions of different doctors and/or different patients, and so on.

THE SURGERY

This is the location into which you will inquire. Your research interest may lie in investigating

- the doctor–patient consultation within the wider context of the surgery;
- how consultations are viewed by different staff and in comparison with other facilities the surgery offers to its patients;
- the demands consultations make upon doctors, nurses and support staff;
- how one surgery compares with others locally, and so on.

Why not try writing a similar checklist for the other two scenarios we mentioned – the picket line and the ICT suite? What might your research focus be in relation to each of the activities, actors and locations comprising those two fictitious social situations? Better still, try the same exercise in relation to a social situation of your own choosing; one which you may already be contemplating researching. This should help to sharpen your research focus, and it may also help you to develop further the questions which will be the foundation of your investigations. Although all three elements – activities, actors and locations – are related and you will always find a degree of overlap, you will see that, by and large, your own research topics may more naturally fall into one of the three components of any social situation. Focus on which of the three best suits your own research interests and you will make your research manageable.

Gaining access and establishing yourself

Once you have decided on the social situation you will explore or once you have, at the very least, a rough idea of what you want to research, what should you do? Your first task is to gain permission to conduct your study in your preferred setting. Remember, no matter how interested and enthusiastic you appear, or how well-supported you are by your university, college, employer or research-funder, you are asking permission to partake in private matters. This means that you should approach with respect those who are in a position to grant or refuse you access. Prepare a letter explaining the purpose of your research and why your chosen setting would benefit your study. Include in your letter assurances and guarantees that any information collected would be used purely in the interests of the research project and for no other purpose. Explain the benefits for the participants of granting you access: what's in it for them? Reassure them that they will have access to all research findings. Offer to discuss with them any reservations they might have, preferably in person. Include professional or character references or a letter of introduction from a third party if you think it would be helpful.

We admit that whenever we have conducted observational studies, most notably in classrooms and other school-based settings, we have always enjoyed the luxury of the total support of our employers – whether university departments or independent research organizations. Consequently, their reputations for integrity and trustworthiness have preceded us. This undoubtedly helps gain entry to social settings, but the principle remains the same even if you are out on your own: be respectful; gain and keep the trust placed in you; be open and transparent in your actions; and keep your promises.

Sometimes, however, all of this will not be enough and permission will be refused. Try not to despair if this happens. Remember, your research is likely to be far more important to you than to anyone else. Prepare in advance for this eventuality by compiling a shortlist of suitable potential settings, and if at first you don't succeed . . .

Once you have gained access, how do you enter your setting on your first day of data collection without disrupting everything and forcing everyone to stop, turn their heads towards you and stare wondering who this stranger is among them. People are naturally curious, generally flattered but occasionally suspicious about why you are there. To make your entrance more comfortable we recommend you prepare in advance a basic, friendly, down-to-earth way of introducing yourself and your research project. Even if your research subjects had been told of your impending visit and a little about your research, they will appreciate hearing from you in person, and this will provide an opportunity to break the ice and get to know one another. In our experience, whatever you say should be truthful, though it does no harm to be a little vague – for example: 'We're just looking at . . .' or 'We're keen to understand how you . . .'. A vague summary of your research is far less intimidating than a jargon-filled detailed description, especially if you feel your subjects might interpret your research to be a judgemental or critical look at their attitudes and behaviour or at the organisation in which they work.

Over time, you will get to know the particular setting you are observing, the people occupying it, and their routines and roles. The longer you stay, or the more visits you make, the deeper your knowledge of these things will become, and the less your presence will influence them. Early on, your priority should be simply to familiarise yourself with the setting you are studying. This will mean getting acquainted with 'insiders' and developing trusting and co-operative relationships with them. Jorgensen (1989) suggests that it is through such relationships that you will be better able to gain access to important aspects of people's daily lives in your chosen setting, and more likely to be provided and trusted with important information. Although there can be no guarantees, here are a few tips for establishing and maintaining rapport which we have developed from our own experience of conducting observational studies:

BE UNOBTRUSIVE

You are trying to fit in, so try not to stand out. Behave, dress and speak in ways which do not draw attention to yourself. Try to be non-threatening in your questioning and non-judgemental in your demeanour.

BE HONEST

Be open and transparent with people. Answer their questions in ways which put them at their ease. Assure them that the research data will be treated confidentially and participants' identities will be anonymised.

BE UNASSUMING

In planning your research you may have gained considerable knowledge of the kind of setting you now find yourself in. If so, play it down. People may find it unsettling or threatening. You are there not to impress them but to learn from them.

BE A GOOD LISTENER

Listen to the language people use in the setting, become familiar with when and how they use particular terms, and be prepared to use them yourself. They may be used in ways which have a meaning or significance different from those which you might expect.

BE APPROACHABLE

Appearing aloof and detached will do you no favours. By being friendly, approachable and willing to discuss common interests and shared experiences outside the subject matter of your research, you are more likely to be accepted.

As time passes you will gradually establish yourself within the setting you are researching, hopefully becoming less of a stranger to the group and more a member of it. You should gradually stop merely watching the events going on around you and begin to participate or share in them. It is when participation becomes possible that *observation* begins for real.

How to observe: telling the story

So just how should you undertake this complex research exercise called observation? We have always found it helpful to set ourselves six questions (adapted from Goetz and LeComte 1984) – who, what, when, where, why and how – and we recommend you do the same. These are all the elements needed to tell the story of what you see going on around you. It may also be useful to bear in mind the terminology commonly used in telling your story: *acts* are the single actions people do; *activities* are sets of related acts; and *events* are sets of related activities (Spradley 1980: 78). So, by way of an example, a doctor might perform the *act* of writing a prescription, during the *activity* of holding a consultation with a patient, which takes place during his diabetes clinic – the *event*. Let us take each of these six questions in turn:

WHO IS PRESENT?

How would you describe them? What role(s) are they playing? When and how do they enter and leave the setting? Where in the setting do they stand or sit? Why are they there? What effect does their presence have on others? What emotions are they expressing? Are there people present who you would not normally expect to see?

How are people behaving? What are they doing and saying? How does this activity begin and end? Which acts occur routinely? What happens which is out of the ordinary, or is unexpected? Who is involved in this activity and what part does each play? How do they manage to make it happen? What problems do they encounter? Do individuals define the same activity differently?

How does it relate to the activities which occur beforehand or afterwards, or to other events? How long does it last? Would you expect this to happen now? Can and does this happen at regular times or does it occur randomly? What makes now the right or wrong time for this activity? When this happens what else happens at the same time?

What part does the location contribute to what is happening? Is there a specific area of this location which is more or less important than others? If so, what is it and why? Can and does the event happen elsewhere?

What precipitated this activity? Does everyone recognise why this activity is happening and agree that it should be happening now? Why does it happen in this way and not in some other way?

How are the separate acts in this activity organised? Do some acts occur before others? Are there rules or norms operating? How do people recognise that this is an instance of this activity?

Trying to juggle the two tasks of carefully observing your surroundings and simultaneously recording what you see in written form, either in prose or more systematically, is a difficult skill to master. But you will get better with practice. In order to help develop the habit and skill of (successfully) recording your observations, there are two tricks of the trade which we recommend you try out.

Our first is the *fieldwork diary*. We have found fieldwork diaries to be indispensable, and cannot recommend them highly enough. They can be used to plan the dates of all your observation sessions, to record the amount of time you have spent in the setting you are researching, to log when major events take place, to review who has and has not been interviewed, to book appointments to conduct further interviews, and to see which locations you have observed the most and the least. In fact, a research diary is a complete historical record of the data-collection phase of your observational research project; something which will prove invaluable when you eventually come to write up your research.

Our second tip is to use a *framework* or *checklist* based on the questions in the 'Telling the story' section above. You should carry your checklist with you throughout each observation session to remind you of what it is you should be attending to. Depending on your approach, the checklist should help you either to organize your more descriptive written notes, or to inform the design of a systematically structured observation schedule. We reproduce one such framework in Box 5.2 for you to use or adapt to your own requirements, and outline these two approaches in the section which follows.

BOX 5.2 Observation framework checklist

- ◆ *space*: the physical place or places
- ◆ *actor*: the people involved
- ◆ *activity*: a set of related acts people do
- ◆ *object*: the physical things which are present
- ◆ *act*: single actions which people do
- ◆ *event*: a set of related activities which people carry out
- ◆ *time*: the sequencing which takes place over time
- ◆ *goal*: the things people are trying to accomplish
- ◆ *feeling*: the emotions felt and expressed

(Spradley 1980: 78)

Capturing what you see

All observation strategies possess two basic features – what is to be observed, and how it is to be recorded. You may by now have realised that deciding what to observe is not as straightforward as you expected it to be. A whole variety of options awaits you as you prepare to set foot in your research setting. How to record what you observe is another decision you will have to make and, once again, there are choices to be made. Broadly speaking, there are two approaches to recording your observations: a *structured* approach and a *descriptive* approach. The first involves the systematic counting of events and their relationships, while the second attempts to look beyond such measures to explore the meanings of events. The two are very different, but not mutually exclusive. You can choose one of the two approaches or combine elements of both in your own research inquiries, depending on your personal preference. What exactly does each entail?

A STRUCTURED APPROACH: SYSTEMATIC OBSERVATION

How long did the doctor's consultation last? How many pupils read to the teacher during the lesson? How long did the nurse spend with each of the patients on her ward? Did male or female shoppers make the most purchases of this particular product? How many arrests did the duty sergeant deal with today, and with what offences were those arrested charged? There are many questions about quantities in social settings and, therefore, a number of ways of quantifying what happens in them. Nevertheless, they all share a common characteristic: because the aim is to determine how often or to what extent some activity or event occurs within the social setting being studied, it is necessary to have already decided what is to be quantified – in other words, the *structure* of your observation. You can make these decisions carefully in advance, and that may make your observation sessions a less stressful experience. On the other hand, it may make it harder for you to respond to unexpected events or to adjust the focus of your research; so build in a little flexibility. The checklist in Box 5.2 may help you to decide which elements of your setting you will concentrate upon.

Once you have decided which feature(s) of your chosen social setting you will observe, you should then devise a list of categories of behaviour (in the case of people) or activities (in the case of locations) which are of particular interest to you and your research project and that you intend to quantify. For example, if the purpose of your study is to examine some aspects of teachers' behaviour in their classrooms, for each observation session you undertake you may want to focus on how teachers divide up their time in setting tasks, how they monitor their pupils' work, how they hold class discussions, how they manage unruly behaviour, and so on. Perhaps, instead, you are interested in how often and with which of her pupils the teacher engages in different kinds of dialogue, such as asking questions, giving commands or instructions, or praising and criticising. Alternatively, if your research interest lies with pupils' behaviour, you may choose to focus on a single pupil, a small group or a whole class, depending on the purpose of your study. How many categories you should devise is really up to you. Too many and it may prove difficult for you to record systematically the whole range of behaviours in which you are interested. You may find yourself shuffling through your papers looking for just the right category and missing all kinds of events and interactions as a result. Too few and you risk subsuming qualitatively different behaviours into a single overly general category. A category like 'pupil concentrating', for example, tells us nothing about the object of the pupil's concentration: the teacher's instructions? the task he has been set? his neighbour's conversation? the football match he can see going on outside?

A research project, reported by Simpson and Tuson (1995), which examined individual pupils' disruptive behaviour in class, used a very simple structured observation schedule. The researchers devised in advance five categories of learning-avoidance behaviour. Each category formed one row of a structured observation schedule. The researchers observed one pupil at a time. Each observation lasted thirty minutes – the duration of a single lesson. Only one observation was conducted per day, and each took place in a different lesson so that a pupil's disruptive behaviour in a mathematics lesson could be compared with his or her behaviour in a languages lesson, and a music lesson, and so on. Each session formed one column of the schedule. The observer simply tallied how often each of the five types of behaviour occurred over the course of each lesson. The completed schedule is reproduced in Figure 5.1.

Tally-based observation schedules are perhaps among the easier and more straightforward event-recording instruments. Their simple purpose is to make frequency counts of particular acts, and they do their job well. Even in the example in Figure 5.1, you can see how many times this particular pupil engages in each of the five types of disruptive behaviour over the course of a single lesson. But you can also easily discern which he engages in most and least often, as well as which lessons are associated with his best and worst behaviour, how he behaves at different times of the day, and on different days of the week. Furthermore, by using the same schedule, John Smith's behaviour patterns can be easily compared with those of other disruptive pupils. As Simpson and Tuson concluded (1995: 30), 'such information might form a basis for identifying patterns of learning or behavioural difficulties associated with different contexts and planning a programme to improve matters'. However, this simple design is not without its weaknesses. In the above example, even if we accept that the five categories of disruptive behaviour in the schedule were sufficient to describe adequately every

John Smith	Date 20/2 Time 10.05 Duration 30 mins Subject Maths	Date 22/2 Time 11.35 Duration 30 mins Subject Language	Date 24/2 Time 3.00 Duration 30 mins Subject Music
Twisting or clenching hands	⊦⊦⊦⊦ ⊦⊦⊦⊦ ⊦⊦⊦⊦ III	⊦⊦⊦⊦ ⊦⊦⊦⊦ ⊦⊦⊦⊦ ⊦⊦⊦⊦ III	
Rocking body/head	⊦⊦⊦⊦ III	⊦⊦⊦⊦ ⊦⊦⊦⊦ I	I
Distracting neighbours	⊦⊦⊦⊦ ⊦⊦⊦⊦ III	⊦⊦⊦⊦ III	
Making nonsense sounds: humming, talking to self	III	⊦⊦⊦⊦ III	
Thumb-sucking	⊦⊦⊦⊦ II	III	II

FIGURE 5.1 A tally system of recording observations (Adapted from Simpson and Tuson 1995: 29)

instance of John Smith's bad behaviour, we cannot tell precisely when in a lesson he began and ended each instance of his disruptive behaviour. Neither can we tell to what or whom his behaviour was a response, nor what the teacher was doing or what else was happening in the classroom at the same time, nor the order (if any) in which he engaged in the five types of activity.

More advanced category-based structured observation schedules have been developed in response to the limitations and disadvantages of basic event-recording schedules such as the tally-based example in Figure 5.1. Perhaps the most widely used, at least in educational research, is Flanders's Interaction Analysis Categories (FIAC). Originally developed more than thirty years ago (Flanders 1970), the FIAC system has been consistently used, with minor refinements, to examine verbal interactions between teachers and pupils. It has proven to be a very popular research instrument among both qualified and trainee teachers keen to analyse their own teaching practices or those of their colleagues. For these reasons FIAC deserves to be described in some detail here (Box 5.3) but we would encourage those of you for whom classroom-based inquiry is not your primary focus to see the merits of FIAC for studying interactions between people in many different social settings, and adapt the FIAC approach to fit in with your own research interests.

BOX 5.3 The ten FIAC categories

---

1   *Accepts feelings* of pupils in a non-threatening manner. Feelings may be positive or negative. Predicting and recalling feelings are included.

2   *Praises or encourages* pupil action or behaviour, including jokes which release tension, nodding head or saying 'Uh-uh' or 'Go on.'

3   *Accepts or uses ideas of pupils*, including clarifying, building or developing pupils' ideas or suggestions. As teacher refers more to their own ideas, shift to category 5.

4   *Asks a question* of pupil about content or procedure with the intent that the pupil should answer.

5   *Lectures* about content or procedure, including giving facts or opinions, expressing own ideas or asking rhetorical questions.

6   *Gives directions*, commands or orders with which a pupil is expected to comply.

7   *Criticises or justifies authority* with the intention of changing pupil behaviour from unacceptable to acceptable pattern.

8   *Student talk – response*: talk by pupil in response to teacher. Teacher initiates contact or solicits pupil statement.

9   *Student talk – initiation*: talk by pupil which he or she initiate. Pupil wants to talk if permitted or called upon by teacher.

10 *Silence or confusion* in which communication cannot be understood by the observer.

(Adapted from Flanders 1970: 34)

To use the FIAC system you first need to acquaint yourself with the ten categories of teacher–pupil interaction in Box 5.3. Then, for each observation session you undertake, you should follow this sequence of four steps (adapted from Wragg 1999: 38–9):

1   Take your FIAC observation schedule with you (see Figure 5.2). The schedule has rows of twenty squares available for each minute of time. Every three seconds the category number is recorded which best describes what is taking place; for example, 4 for a teacher's question, 8 for a pupil's reply.

2   Record across the schedule so that each line represents one minute of observation time.

3   Identify separate episodes, such as 'setting a task', 'monitoring pupils' work', or 'summarising the lesson', in the margin so it is clear what kinds of acts occur during different activities, and which activities comprise the lesson as a whole.

4   Use a stopwatch or the second hand of a wristwatch to remind you to record
    a category every three seconds.

FIAC DATA SHEET

School _____   Teacher _____

Class _____   Subject/topic _____

Date _____   Observer _____

(Tally across)

01																				
02																				
03																				
04																				
05																				
06																				
07																				
08																				
09																				
10																				
11																				
12																				
13																				
14																				
15																				
16																				
17																				
18																				
19																				
20																				
21																				
22																				
23																				
24																				
25																				
26																				
27																				
28																				
29																				
30																				

FIGURE 5.2 FIAC observation schedule

In practice, therefore, your observation schedule will contain sequences of numbers, to be read from left to right, top to bottom. Take the example of fictitious teacher–pupil dialogue in Box 5.4 by way of illustration:

BOX 5.4 Example of teacher–pupil talk

Teacher:	Stop writing, please!	6 (command)
	Listen!	6 (command)
	Who has managed to finish their story?	4 (question)
	(*six second pause*)	10 (silence)
		10 (silence)
Pupil 1:	I have, Mr Jones.	8 (solicited pupil talk)
	(*three second pause*)	10 (silence)
Pupil 2:	I'm having problems with the ending.	9 (pupil-initiated talk)
Teacher:	That's nothing to worry about.	1 (accepts feelings)
	I think you've done extremely well to get that far. Well done!	2 (praise)

The observer would record this 30-second exchange on the observation schedule as shown in Figure 5.3.

08	6	6	4	10	10	8	10	9	1	2										

FIGURE 5.3 FIAC schedule showing a 30-second exchange

A thirty-minute observation session, with an entry made every three seconds, will yield 600 separate entries (if you can keep up!), which will allow a whole variety of quantitative statements to be made simply by counting the number of times each category is selected. A simple analysis of frequency would provide you with information relating to a number of factors, listed in Box 5.5, and there would be nothing to stop the more confident researchers among you from subjecting your data to more complex and advanced statistical analysis.

Despite the rigorous and systematic nature of structured observation schedules, some aspects of social settings are problematical or even impossible to quantify. How would we measure the atmosphere in the classroom during a lesson we were observing, or how well (or otherwise) pupils understand what their teacher wishes them to do, for example? How would we tell, from looking at a FIAC schedule, whether the observed lesson was enjoyable for the pupils,

BOX 5.5 Simple FIAC analysis

The number of/the average length of/the amount of time taken up by

- teacher's utterances
- pupils' utterances
- statements of approval or disapproval
- reprimands
- episodes, e.g. introducing the lesson, setting a task, discussing a topic
- silences, pauses or disruptions, and so on

The percentage of:

- talk and non-talk
- teacher-talk and pupil-talk
- questions and answers, and so on

rewarding or frustrating for the teacher, even simply a good or bad lesson, typical or out of the ordinary? To answer questions like these we need to adopt a qualitative rather than quantitative approach to our observations; one which seeks to describe and understand rather than categorise what we see going on around us.

A DESCRIPTIVE APPROACH: WRITING FIELD NOTES

Perhaps surprisingly, most field notes are not written in the field. They are an expanded account of all kinds of information you might obtain during your observation session and which you assemble after the event. One major source of information is jottings. Remember, one of the golden rules we outlined earlier is to be unobtrusive, and you are unlikely to remain so if you spend most of your session furiously scribbling down notes. So, instead, subtly jot down phrases, summaries, short sentences, abbreviations, even just one or two key words which you feel capture interesting aspects of what you see. Afterwards, when you come to write up your field notes in full, your jottings will trigger your memory of the event. A small notebook is ideal. A dictaphone or mini-disc-recorder and microphone may work well if you are not a keen scribbler (though it may be advisable to use it in a noisy setting and to speak quietly!). Lap-top computers may be too conspicuous, but, interestingly, we are seeing palm-held computers, which have the added advantage of enabling notes to be transferred quickly and conveniently into files on a PC, increasingly used. What you record and how you record are matters of personal preference. There are no hard and fast rules.

Experiment a little, and soon you will develop a jottings' style which best jogs your memory later on.

By way of illustration, Figure 5.4 contains an exact reproduction of jottings we recently made during an observation session from a real research project designed to investigate the ways in which secondary-school-aged children might

---

Macbeth Storyboard Classroom Trials – Observation schedule

NAME OF SCHOOL   BLACKBERRY SCHOOL

NAME OF TEACHER   CHRIS DAY

CLASS   YR 10 MIXED ABILITY n = 23

DATE   29 / 3 / 00

Room layout, including position and direction of video camera, number and position of desks, pupils, chalkboard, gender of pupils etc.

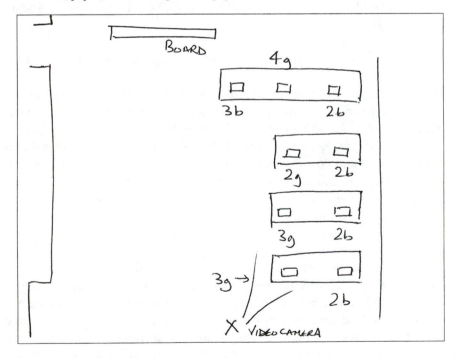

TIME	TEACHER'S ACTIONS Inc. lesson intro. Beginning and end of tasks, movement around classroom, conclusion of lesson	PUPILS' ACTIONS Inc. concentration levels, movement around classroom, grouping, reactions to teacher, questioning
11.40 – 11.50	10 minute introduction and explanation of task.	All on task. Extremely wide variety of interpretations – backgrounds, size of character, prop, posture of character. Use of visual and text windows.
11.50 – 12.15	Own assessment of groups: walking from grp to grp asking Q's relating to storyboard construction. ↓	No discernable difference in behaviour between b+g (1 grp of 4 g a little excited). Abundance of group discussion and decision-making. Pointing and positioning with hands.
12.15 – 12.25	T groups class around grps presenting their work. |SHEPHERDING| pupils into semi-circle around computer.	2 × 5 min. sessions: 2 all-girl grps, explain reasons for construction of frames: text posture of characters character moods Atmosphere All observers silent and attentive.

FIGURE 5.4 Reproduction of a descriptive observation schedule

use a piece of state-of-the-art software – a computer program called *Kar2ouche*[1] – for their study of William Shakespeare's *Macbeth* (for a detailed account of an in-depth video-based follow-up study to this project, see Chapter 6). The jottings were written on an observation schedule we had prepared in advance of observing the software in use in a real lesson at a school which had agreed to trial the program. The schedule was designed so that the duration of the lesson acted as a baseline against which to record the events and activities the teacher and his pupils engaged in. Incorporated into the schedule was the space to label the session clearly and to draw a diagram of the classroom, including objects and people within it, and a reminder of potentially significant activities we should try to record. For any of the pupils' actions it is possible to see what the teacher was doing at the same time (and vice versa), as well as approximately how long into the lesson each occurred. The design of the schedule is such that it is flexible enough to be used not only in classrooms, but in all kinds of settings where people interact with one another over a period of time. Please feel free to use or adapt it for your own research purposes.

You will see that the jottings incorporate summaries, key words and abbreviations of a kind we recommend you use yourself. For example, you can see the teacher's '10 minute introduction and explanation of task' during which time the pupils were 'all on task', that among the pupils there was 'no discernible difference in behaviour between b + g (1 grp of 4 g a little excited)', and that the teacher's organisation of his pupils into a semi-circle was described vividly as 'shepherding.'

The field notes you compile will be the core of your observational study and the foundation for the analysis phase of your research. They should therefore be as complete and accurate as possible. This requirement can extend your field notes to many more pages than you had originally anticipated, especially if you combine extended accounts of your jottings with transcripts of your interviews, diagrams, photographs and even video-recordings of the setting, and other useful contextualising documents. To manage your data it is important that your field notes are well constructed and well organised. To help you achieve this we advise you to:

- *Write your notes as soon as possible after the observation.* The longer you wait, the greater the risk of forgetting important details. Schedule writing-up time in your research diary, and stick to it! One hour of observation can easily take three or four times longer to write up, so allocate sufficient time. Why do yourself the disservice of conducting a meticulous observation session only to produce a poor, overly-rushed set of field notes?

- *Label your notes properly.* Reserve spaces for noting the name of the observer, the date, location and time of the observation session, as well as a useful title to help you to recall the session.

- *Leave plenty of space*. In the margins supplement your notes with hunches, thoughts, issues, reminders, emerging patterns, further questions you would like to ask, and so on. Do not be afraid to start new paragraphs. Any new event or activity you observe deserves a new paragraph. This will make your notes easy to read and, later, to analyse.
- *Write first, edit later*. However tempted you are to organise your notes around emerging themes or topics, please resist. Record them instead according to the chronological flow of the session and wait until you have completed your notes, and notes relating to other sessions, before you return to them to edit or re-organise them thematically. You need to step back and see the bigger picture before you can detect important topics and issues.

Figure 5.5 contains an extract from the final report of the research project, mentioned above, which investigated the use of software to study *Macbeth*. This extract is comprised of the field notes relating to one trial lesson observed and recorded using the schedule in Figure 5.4. We were able to draw upon many sources of information in writing the field notes, including video-recordings of the class at work, audio-recordings both of the teacher setting his task and of the pupils' conversations and presentations to the class, transcripts of interviews with the teacher and his pupils, and the computer files containing the pupils' finished work. Just as important as all of these, however, were the original jottings reproduced in Figure 5.4.

The extract in Figure 5.5 has its origins in the jottings in Figure 5.4. Without them we would have found it a great deal harder to write these field notes and, in turn, the final report to which this extract contributed. In the final report, this account of a single lesson was combined with accounts of three other lessons with classes in different schools in which we trialled the *Kar2ouche* software. All four accounts, along with all the supporting material we had gathered, were combined and analysed in ways we discuss in Chapters 2 and 4 to identify emerging themes, issues and topics for further research (Birmingham and Davies 2001). They included, for example, pupils' progress and motivation to learn, the nature of their interactions with each other and with the computer, the user-friendliness of the software, factors in its successful integration with classroom activities, and the demand it placed upon schools' existing ICT facilities. We recommend that you turn to these chapters for ideas about how to analyse your field notes using qualitative methods.

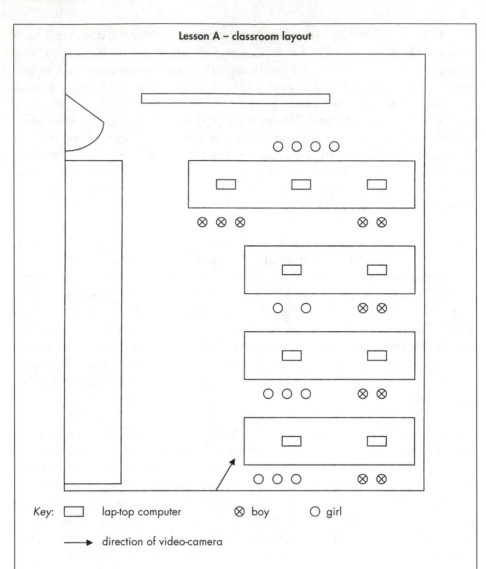

Lesson A – classroom layout

Key: ▭ lap-top computer   ⊗ boy   ○ girl

⟶ direction of video-camera

Lesson A

The lesson began with a ten-minute introduction during which the teacher explained the task he had set his pupils. Using rough pen-and-paper storyboards, prepared prior to the lesson for guidance, the pupils were given twenty-five minutes to complete between four and six storyboard frames, including backgrounds, characters and text, jotting down notes to explain the choices and the decisions they had made and practising reading the lines they had selected to accompany each frame.

The teacher asked his pupils especially to bear in mind what their choice of backgrounds might suggest to the audience viewing the finished storyboards, how they should position the characters and what their choice of position might reveal about the characters' states of mind or their relationships with each other, which key lines of the scene best fit with each frame, and how those lines should be spoken.

The teacher informed pupils of his intention to assess orally some of the groups as they read aloud their interpretations of the scene and explained the decisions and choices they had made. He then said he would be asking groups to volunteer to present their work to the rest of the class at the end of the lesson.

Throughout the twenty-five minute task all the groups of pupils, apart from one group of four girls who were occasionally distracted and excited, concentrated hard on their work. A great deal of discussion and debate seemed to take place within, and sometimes between, groups, with individual pupils drawing on paper copies of the text of the scene and their paper storyboards to reinforce their points to group members. All groups seemed to make full use of both the visual and text windows of Kar2ouche[1], alternating between them regularly. There was also a great deal of pointing at, and gesturing towards, the computer screens in pupils' efforts to communicate to their groups what they wanted to be happening on screen.

While pupils were working the teacher stopped at each group in turn to listen closely to their discussions and to ask questions relating to the construction of their storyboards and their choice of accompanying text.

In the remaining ten minutes of the lesson two groups presented their work for five minutes each to the rest of the class, who, shepherded by the teacher, gathered in rough semi-circles around each group's lap-top computer. The presentations are reported below.

FIGURE 5.5 Trial lesson field notes

Conclusion

Observation is not a research method which suits everyone. It can consume a great deal of a researcher's time and energy, and the reward for investing all that effort can be a long time coming. Yet observation can be one of the most professionally gratifying experiences a researcher can have. To see what is *actually* going on in the social setting you are researching – which may not at all be what you are accustomed to seeing or what you expected or presumed you would see – is both the challenge and the reward of observational research. With careful planning and a little practice there is no reason why you should not be up to that challenge.

Note

1   *Kar2ouche* is a registered trademark of Immersive Education Ltd.:
      http://www.kar2ouche.com

Key texts on observational research

For those new to research

Robson, C. (1993) 'Observational methods', Chapter 8 of *Real World Research*, Oxford: Blackwell.

The chapter in which Colin Robson discusses observation is a particularly accessible and friendly introduction to the major issues associated with this research method. He sets out clearly the main advantages and disadvantages of observational research, the various approaches available to the researcher, how to get started and how to analyse the data. This chapter would be the perfect first port of call as you set out on your observational study.

For the intermediate researcher

Lofland, J. and Lofland, L.H. (1995) *Analysing Social Settings*, 3rd edition, Belmont, CA: Wadsworth.

This user-friendly theoretically-focused text builds on many of the issues covered in Robson's *Real World Research*, adopting a similar style while discussing much more extensively the three crucial ingredients of observational research: gathering, focusing and analysing data. The book also contains a thorough treatment of coding using computers, and useful chapters on writing reports and dissecting others' observations.

For the expert

Fetterman, D.M. (1998) *Ethnography*, 2nd edition, London: Sage.

This pocket-sized text disguises a wealth of advanced, yet clearly written, information about the process of conducting ethnographic research. As well as discussing in depth issues surrounding the nature of fieldwork, qualitative and quantitative data analysis, and writing research reports, this title is one of the first (and best) to consider the 'new frontier' of observational research – the internet. The author discusses the potential provided by this new medium for research in relation to conducting searches, collecting and sharing data, using online journals and listservs, and downloading data-collection and analysis software.

Researching the things people say and do: an alternative approach to research

In this chapter we:

This final chapter considers another research instrument you may wish to employ in your own research: the video-camera. But, as it is the last chapter of the book, we would also like to use what we say about this particular research instrument to introduce you to a genuinely alternative way of approaching the *whole research process*, from start to finish – one that has been called a *reverse strategy* by its practitioners, and which has been made possible only by the advent of, first, the tape-recorder and, more recently, the video-camera.

The video-camera

The video-camera is not intrinsically a research instrument. Neither are its audio-only counterparts, the humble tape-recorder and the more high-tech mini-disc-recorder. None of these was invented as a tool with which to conduct research and none was designed with the researcher in mind. Nevertheless, the tape-recorder has been enthusiastically adopted by great swathes of the research community, and the mini-disc-recorder and video-camera are rapidly catching up. We investigated the reasons for this in Chapter 2 in relation to interviews as a research instrument.

No matter how accurately they record interviews, that particular facility does not make audio-recorders and video-cameras research instruments. In those situations, your research instrument is still the *interview itself*, supported by your interview schedule. The interview is the tool you use to obtain your data. These devices simply help you to record and store your interview, albeit extremely reliably. So, these devices need to be used differently if we are to regard them as research instruments in their own right. But can they be used differently and, if so, how?

One other way to use a video-camera, of course, is to take it into a particular environment, set it up, aim it at a group of people and press the record button, having gained permission beforehand of course! Doing this will provide you with a recording of those people in their natural setting, going about their daily business, interacting with one another, and saying and doing a variety of things. Were you to treat such a recording as data, then the video-camera would indeed be the research instrument you used in your collection of that data. But why on earth would you want to do that? How could such data possibly be of any use to you in your research, especially if you entered that environment with few, if any, preconceived notions of what exactly you wanted to research? Would the recording, in fact, be data at all?

Let us look closely at these questions. We think such video-recordings do constitute data, but data of a very distinctive kind. In order to appreciate their distinctiveness we need to think a little differently about what we mean by 'data', and what role data-collection plays in the research process. We will be helped in this by developing an analogy with the archaeologist. We will then distinguish between question-driven and data-driven research strategies to explain the basis of this alternative research approach.

Are researchers 'archaeologists by choice'?

On Channel 4 in the UK there is a long-running popular television programme called *Time Team.* Each episode covers a three-day excavation at a location somewhere in the British Isles in which a group of professional archaeologists uncovers the remains of buildings, fragments of pottery or bone, discarded coins, tools, jewellery and other evidence of human habitation. Piecing all this together with the aid of a traditional artist and the latest computer graphics technology, the team reconstructs a picture of a society long since lost to us. The reconstruction process is a frustrating business, both for the archaeologists and the many experts and assistants on the programme and for the viewers at home. This is because archaeology's central aim is to unlock the secrets of the past and bring to life the way things really were; from complex issues such as how people made their livings, how they tended to their sick and infirm, how they practised their religion and acted in times of war, as well as the simplest, ordinary matters of how they addressed one another, how they interacted and how they would pass the time. Any archaeologist would seize the chance of spending just one day observing the ordinary life of a past civilisation, but they are forced instead to use whatever fragments they can get hold of to recreate a tantalising glimpse of how life might have been.

Back in 1964, the American sociologist Aaron Cicourel described some of his fellow sociologists as 'archaeologists by choice' (Cicourel 1964: 122). He was reminding them of something which seemed to have passed most of them by: that despite the luxury of being able to study society by observing ordinary social life going on around them in places like the classroom, on the hospital ward, in local government offices, on the shop floor, in the city, at the police station, in the laboratory, in the home, on the street, and so on, by and large they chose not to do so. And to this day they prefer instead to do what the archaeologist has no choice but to do: they investigate society not by looking closely at it in all its detail but by deliberately filtering out that detail. They then reconstruct society from isolated fragments such as census and questionnaire results, statistics, tables, graphs, charts, newspapers and diaries. They do this not because it is difficult to research ordinary social life or because they need specialised and sophisticated equipment to do so, but because they find what people say and do ordinarily, routinely, day-in, day-out and as a matter of course of little interest or relevance in the first place.

145

Cicourel's analogy between the sociologist and the archaeologist sums up everything he, along with a considerable number of colleagues and allies in the sociology community then and still to this day, find problematic about researching social life, namely researchers' apparent preoccupation with representing social life in (and reducing it to) a succession of variables, statistics, graphs, charts, tables, survey findings, field notes and other fragments. Just as the only means for archaeologists *truly* to understand an extinct society would be to go back in time, walk the streets, watch as events and activities unfold, and listen to all the conversations going on there, in the same way, so certain researchers contend, we need to study precisely the same fine detail of everyday life in our current society if we are really to increase our understandings of the topics, themes and issues which interest us as researchers.

This alternative research programme which Cicourel advocated and helped formulate came to be known as ethnomethodology. Out of ethnomethodology developed conversation analysis. Both form the bedrock on which we have built this chapter. Many knowledgeable authors have written excellent and accessible introductions to ethnomethodology and conversation analysis, and we provide useful references to their work at the end of this chapter. Please do not let these terms worry you. Put simply, ethnomethodology is the study of how people produce and make sense of the affairs of daily life, in all their fine detail, wherever and however they are carried out. Conversation analysis studies the orderly and organised features of everyday talk – one such affair of daily life – and how talkers themselves achieve, appreciate, and use that orderliness in their conversations.

Researching the detail

Can we, as researchers, be convinced of the value of researching the fine detail of what our subjects say and do? In light of what we have said thus far, to do so would appear to be no mean feat. So, before we ask *how* we can conduct our inquiries into what goes on in our chosen environments, and in ways which preserve rather than filter out all the essential detail, we need to ask ourselves *why* we should bother.

As researchers we will often be interested in researching events, activities, exchanges – things that go on in the world around us, or in a specific environment within it. Your own research interests may lie in education, medicine, law, politics, business or commerce, for example. Within those fields you may be interested in some aspect of teaching and learning, nursing or general practice, crime and justice, sales and marketing, or banking and finance. Those of us for whom research is not our main occupation, but is instead something we undertake occasionally as part of our day job as, say, students, teachers, nurses, council officers, or commercial directors, may be fortunate enough to have privileged access to environments we might want to explore. Educationalists may obtain permission to conduct their research in real classrooms, focusing on teachers as they set tasks, and on pupils' behaviour as they attempt them. Health care professionals conducting research may have access to hospital wards, doctors' rounds or the local surgery. The courts, a local legal practice or a nearby police station may be open to members of the legal profession interested in investigating topics related to crime or the judicial system, and researchers whose professional interests lie in business may have the opportunity to track other key business personnel, to attend boardroom meetings, to be present at negotiations and to watch as important commercial decisions are taken.

These diverse environments, from the classroom to the boardroom and beyond, all have one thing in common: they contain people saying and doing things; people who are (at least some of the time) teachers, pupils, doctors, nurses, patients, policemen, lawyers, judges, suspects, criminals, sales reps, customers, managers and company directors. And they may say and do a bewildering variety of things day-in, day-out, while they play out their roles as teachers, pupils, doctors, and so on. So it is not unreasonable to assume that if you are interested in researching the work practices or the attitudes and beliefs of groups of people like these, they will be found in what they do with, and say to, one another.

But even if we agree that the topics and issues we might want to research 'come to life' in the detail of what it is that particular people in particular contexts say and do, and that detail, therefore, is where we should be looking, should we not at least decide in advance what specifically we want to look at – which questions we want the video-tape to answer – before we begin recording? How can we justify simply entering an environment with a video-camera, pointing it at certain people doing certain things and pressing the record button? The answer lies in this research method's *reverse strategy*, mentioned earlier. By this we mean that research conducted in this manner effectively proceeds in the opposite direction to that of most research you will have read or engaged in. Most research is motivated by a question (or set of related questions), and we hope this book has helped you to equip yourselves with the skills and knowledge required to carry out your research in this way. This alternative method of conducting research, on the other hand, is motivated by what can be seen to be happening when you look: in other words, motivated by data. How does this work in practice?

Normally, after some initial reading, you are likely to begin your research journey with a particular question or set of questions in mind. Armed with your topic or question, you might then ask yourself a number of preparatory questions: Where will you go to investigate and explore your topic? Once you are there what data will you need to collect? How will you collect them? What form should the data take? How will you know when you have enough? Do you need to talk to people? If so, how many should you talk to and for how long? Do you need to ask people questions directly in interviews or would it be better to get them to respond in other ways and by other means, perhaps by questionnaire? Is it enough simply to talk to people or do you need additional supporting information? Then, further down the road, how will you make sense of the data you collect, and what sensible conclusions will you draw from your data?

Although you will be faced with a few twists and turns as you go, by and large the path you take through your research will lead you in one direction, beginning with identifying your question(s), then moving on to collecting your data, and ending with analysing the data you collect. The whole process begins with your research question. Finding an answer by collecting and analysing the right kinds of data is what motivates you as a researcher. All your inquiries are question-driven, and the big question in your mind is *what data do I need to answer this question*?

In adopting a question-driven approach to your research you may be doing more in the earlier stages of your inquiries than merely establishing the question(s) you intend to pursue. To decide on the questions you *will* ask means having to discard or reject many others which you will not. It means deciding on the issues or themes you will explore within the much broader general topic you are interested in researching. Very often you will make those decisions according to how interesting, important or relevant you judge them to be. In short, you decide what is and is not worth researching.

The reverse strategy is to withhold any such decisions. The data, and not the question(s), are what motivate your inquiries. The first thing to do is to go into the environment you are keen to explore and capture what is happening there. This is where the video-camera comes into its own. A video-camera is portable and can be taken almost anywhere. It will record what happens as it happens, in all its original detail. The camera never lies. Unlike researchers, the video-camera cannot make mistakes (though of course it can develop a fault), misinterpret what it records, miss things altogether (as long as they are in shot), or decide for itself which of all the activities and events being recorded are the most important, relevant, interesting or worthy of research. By recording everything in shot, nothing is prioritised. The data which a video-camera provides you with constitute a perfect record of what happened. In the recording are preserved, in all their original detail, the things people were saying and doing at the time. Very little, if anything, is lost. Nothing is deliberately discarded. Nothing is filtered out.

Now that you have your data, they are what you work with – no more, no less. You analyse the data by examining the recording in terms of its detailed and specific features. This will enable you to say what your data actually are: what the events and activities captured on camera actually are, and not what you might have thought they were or even what you might reasonably expect them to be. The analysis will also help you to determine the kinds of things you can say – based on observation, not speculation – about, and on the basis of, the data. It will help you to consider the type(s) of question(s), and how many, you can realistically ask of these data. Or, to put it another way, what question(s) can I solve by using these data? The whole process begins with your data. In research with a reverse strategy, finding a question by collecting and analysing data is what motivates you as a researcher. All your inquiries are data-driven, and the big question in your mind is: *What question can these data answer*? (See Box 6.1 for a summary of the advantages of a data-driven approach.)

BOX 6.1 Merits of the data-driven approach

You will NOT:

♦ be at risk from claiming in your research anything that cannot be legitimately claimed on the basis of your data;

♦ be faced with the problem of having to collect sufficient data of the right sort to answer your research question effectively;

♦ risk asking research questions which are 'out of tune' with the topic or issue you are keen to investigate. You will effectively be allowing the important questions to determine themselves on the basis of what can be seen to be really going on in the situation you are investigating;

♦ have to decide what specifically to focus on and what to discard in your research. Your focus is on your research subjects and on their everyday affairs, one of which may be deciding for themselves what is important, relevant, in need of attention or interesting. Let them decide.

So a central aim of data-driven research is to investigate the things people say and do by closely analysing their actions, activities and conversations which have been captured in their original detail using a video-camera. How exactly can we go about this?

Using video: a case study

The remainder of this chapter takes the form of a case study of one such attempt to use a video-camera as our research instrument. The aim of this particular research project was to investigate the impact on teaching and learning of *Kar2ouche*, a cutting-edge storyboarding software tool developed to enhance pupils' engagement with, and understanding of, complex literary texts such as the plays of William Shakespeare (Birmingham *et al.* 2002). This project was a more detailed and ambitious version of an earlier observational study of *Kar2ouche* mentioned in Chapter 5. Step-by-step, the case study takes you through the stages of the research process, from setting up the video-camera, through the data analysis phase to reaching our conclusions. As well as providing you with an interesting example of data-driven research, we use the case study to frame certain general points and important issues which extend far beyond the subject matter of this particular research project, and which will apply equally to your own projects should you choose to utilise this research method yourself.

Step 1: obtaining your data

The very first thing you must do is to obtain the permission of your subjects (from teachers and/or parents in the case of schoolchildren) to proceed with data collection. Gaining access to social settings may not be straightforward, and we discuss ways to go about this in Chapter 5. Your subjects must be happy with you recording them. It will also mean they must be happy for you to use the recordings in your research project, which may include displaying the recordings in print or at conferences and talks. You should always respect individuals' rights to refuse to consent to this, but it might be possible to minimise the risk of refusal by reassuring your potential participants that the central aim of your research is to observe, describe and understand what they do, and in no way to criticise or judge them. You might also reassure them by guaranteeing to anonymise all your data as far as possible by changing participants' names and the addresses where the recordings are made, and by promising to show any data only to professional audiences.

By now you will understand the importance of collecting video-recordings of people engaged in 'naturally occurring' interactions and conversations. This means collecting recordings of events which in all likelihood would have occurred had you not been present. Of course you can never truly verify that what you have on tape is what would have happened anyway, so in practice the most you can do is to set up your recording equipment to be as unobtrusive as possible, so that it does not prevent your subjects from behaving in 'natural' ways. Box 6.2 offers suggestions on good practice in data collection.

BOX 6.2 Recommendations for successful data collection

♦ Ensure your audio-recording is of sufficient quality to be transcribable. Use an external microphone where possible and place it as near as possible to your subjects. A cheap microphone positioned at the sound source is better than using an expensive microphone located further away or relying on the camera's own internal microphone.

♦ Position your video-camera so your recording contains the people you are interested in researching and provides you with as clear a view as possible of what it is they are doing and any objects or artefacts they are using or to which they may refer. These may include, for example, computer screens, doctors' notes or whiteboards. You may find that two cameras are better than one in this regard.

♦ Use a video-camera that can display the time in the frame on play-back. This will prove invaluable when you come to transcribe your data.

♦ Use a tripod and keep to a fixed position. When you return to look at your data over and over again, you will be glad you recorded a stable image!

♦ Set up your equipment prior to the events you want to record if at all possible, and avoid adjusting and re-adjusting the equipment during recording. Together, this will minimise the intrusion it causes. The intrusion may even be less than that caused by a strange researcher roaming the room!

♦ Bear in mind that the longer the data collection goes on and the more recordings you make, the less impact the camera is likely to have on people's behaviour.

♦ Most importantly, don't expect everything to go without a hitch. Be prepared to revise and amend your practice in light of experience. When you look at your recording ask yourself if there is any way it could be improved upon next time around.

In the *Kar2ouche* project, we spent many lessons trying different set-ups before we decided on the most satisfactory arrangement. This was to place our video-camera behind a pair of pupils so they could not see it without turning round, and film the two of them over the course of many weeks working at a computer on which *Kar2ouche* was installed (see Figure 6.1). We were able to record the pupils interacting with each other (and with the teacher when she appeared in shot), their use of the keyboard and the mouse and their work on the computer screen. In addition, we were able to record the pupils' conversations by means of a small microphone connected to the camera and fixed to the top of their monitor.

FIGURE 6.1 Position of video-camera

Step 2: describing your data

Once you have collected your data your next task is to produce accurate descriptions of them. There is a simple practical reason for this: imagine how impractical and cumbersome it would be if every time you wanted to talk about your research to your colleagues or other professionals you first had to find a video-player and television, or a computer with digitized video-playback facilities. It is also far better to have written transcripts of your recordings which you can then incorporate easily into your research reports. There is also an analytical reason: the activities and events you are keen to explore may be complex and fleeting, and not immediately obvious from one or two viewings of your data. It may take many careful viewings, and many attempts at transcribing the data, before the most interesting or valuable aspects of the data reveal themselves.

Transcripts of video-recordings from data-driven research projects are very different from the kinds of transcriptions you will be familiar with from interview-based research, which, typically, are written versions of what is said during an interview, with any distracting and unnecessary 'noise' removed and perhaps speakers' grammar and slips of the tongue corrected. The process we ourselves have developed and adapted from conversation analytical research using this methodology is a longer one, and is divided into different stages. Although it can be time-consuming we have found it to be extremely helpful in representing our data in finer and finer detail. Here we relate our step-by-step approach using real data from the *Kar2ouche* research project. We recommend you attempt something along these lines in your own projects.

SUMMARISE YOUR DATA

As soon as possible after each data-collection exercise you should watch the tape and write down what is happening in your video-recording. Your task is to produce a basic record or summary of the events you recorded. As you can imagine, the more recordings you make, the more valuable these summaries will become. As you collect more and more data your notes will help you in future to search for specific events, activities or conversations you might wish to examine more closely. At this stage you should not worry about the detail, but each summary should contain at least a title, information about the occasion of the recording such as the date, time and place (so you can link your summary with your original video-recording), and timings of the events you are summarising (so you can locate them easily on the original tape). You may also wish to add extra contextualising information such as a diagram of the room layout showing the location of the video-camera and the direction in which it was pointing, tables, chairs, doorways, your participants, and so on.

Figure 6.2 contains an extract from one of the data summaries we compiled during the *Kar2ouche* project. To put these events into context, Rachel, the teacher, had stopped to see the work our pair of pupils (L, on the left, and R, on the right) had completed using *Kar2ouche*. The software enables pupils to construct visual images of Shakespeare's *Macbeth* using different computer-generated backgrounds, characters and props. Pupils can attach to the characters speech and thought bubbles in which they can insert any text they choose, including extracts from the play itself. They can also type any notes they wish into a caption box under each image or frame. Rachel had already asked her pupils to type in each caption box their reasons for constructing their frames in the way they had, but when Rachel looked at this particular pair's work she noticed that they had started to construct their third frame before typing anything in the previous frame's caption box.

[CTC0305-Rachel-INTEL19-2]

Teacher monitors pupils' work

13:38:20   Rachel looks over R's shoulder. They show her what they have done.

13:38:27   *Rachel*:   Okay.
           L (to R):   You need to write why we thought that in the second frame.
           R: Oh yeah.

13:38:36   *Rachel*:   You haven't put that down?
           L: No

13:38:43   *Rachel (pointing with the finger at the caption box)*:   You need to put your reason down here, don't you?
           L: Yeah.
           (*Rachel goes away.*)

13:38:47   (*L begins to type.*)
           R: Uh, he's just basically scared.
           (*L types*): 'Macbeth is scared of who is there'.

FIGURE 6.2 Data summary extract

In this example we have on the first line the title of the video-recording from which this 30-second extract was taken. Although it is not obvious to the general reader it tells us the date the recording was made, the name of the teacher whose class we were researching (changed to protect her identity), the particular computer and the pupils on whom we were focusing. In the next line we have a (centred) heading describing the events which then follow. The timings of these events are logged down the left-hand side, the events are summarised and a basic transcript of the conversation between the pupils and their teacher is given. The whole summary runs to many pages, as it covers the entire lesson, but even from this short extract you begin to get an impression of what was happening during the thirty seconds the teacher spent with the two pupils we were studying.

In the *Kar2ouche* project we became interested in looking closely at how teachers and pupils interacted around the computer screen. But, in line with data-driven research policy, we became interested in this only *after* having witnessed many lessons during which it became apparent that such events seemed to impact greatly on teaching and learning using technology, and only *after* we had compiled our summaries of all those lessons.

PREPARE AN INITIAL TRANSCRIPT

Your data summary is fine as a way to sum up what your data comprises, but it would be wrong to think of your summaries *as* data. As with our concern with teacher–pupil interaction, your summaries will enable you to locate easily particular events, or types of event, you would like to explore in detail from across all the occasions on which you collected your data. Once you have consulted your summaries to find when these events took place, you should then return to your video-recordings, for *they are* your data. The second step is then to produce an initial transcript of these specific events – which may last anything from a few seconds to many minutes – from your recordings.

Data-driven research in the conversation analysis mould strives to preserve in its transcripts all the fine detail of the original audio- or video-recordings. As Box 6.3 illustrates, this means preserving and displaying both *what* is said and *how* it is said.

This extent of detail in the transcript is necessary in order to provide a full and faithful rendering of all the features of the talk – not just the words themselves – captured in the video-recordings. As researchers, we cannot tell at the outset of our analysis which of all these features might have real implications for our subjects' actions and interactions, so it would be wrong for us to conclude that they are unimportant and can be filtered out. Instead, we must make efforts to preserve them. Many of these features are represented in transcripts by specific symbols such as colons, dashes, brackets, arrows, degree signs, and so on. Together they form a transcription system that has come to be regarded as the definitive

BOX 6.3   Features of talk depicted in conversation analysis transcripts

---

♦ Words as they sound when spoken in contrast to words in their grammatically correct form, for example 'missiz' as opposed to 'Mrs'.

♦ Other, non-verbal, sounds such as laughter, audible breathing, 'tutting', and agreements like 'Uh-huh'.

♦ Inaudible or incomprehensible words, usually by the insertion of empty brackets at the appropriate point.

♦ Pauses or silences in the talk, usually represented in seconds or even fractions of a second.

♦ Overlapped talk or instances where more than one person is speaking at once.

♦ Other features such as intonation, the loudness of the talk, the emphasis or stress on particular words, the speed at which a person speaks, and so on.

---

standard within this type of research. It was developed originally by Gail Jefferson, a pioneer of conversation analysis, and you can find a neat and accessible summary of her system in Appendix A of ten Have (1999).

We have reproduced in Figure 6.3 our initial transcript of the events which occurred (an extract from which is given in Box 6.2), including explanatory remarks about some of the conversation analysis transcription conventions we used in order to try to keep the detail of the events intact.

Although transcripts certainly appear complicated and are time-consuming to produce, we hope you can see the merits of producing a record with this degree of detail. The intention is to provide the reader with a more faithful, more complete, impression of all the various activities which occurred in your original data than would be possible with either a summary or even a conventional interview-style transcript. Our advice is to tackle this process in small stages (see Box 6.4).

At the end of step 2, you should have an accurate and detailed record of what your research participants' say to one another (as well as how it is said) during episodes you have chosen to investigate more thoroughly. But what about the actions of the participants when they were speaking? Remember, the title of this chapter specifies *the things people say and do*, but up to now, compared with the detail of the speech element of your initial transcript, you will have described the other activities going on only superficially. For example, the last line of our transcript, '((starts typing))', contains hardly any detail at all. Step 3,

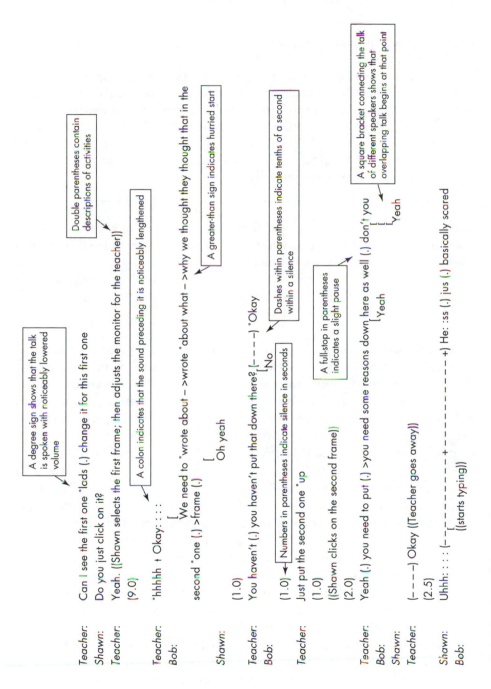

FIGURE 6.3 Initial transcript

BOX 6.4   Step-by-step stages in producing transcripts

---

1   Transcribe the talk as you hear it and not necessarily in its grammatically correct form.
2   Look out for talk which overlaps or coincides with other speech.
3   Listen carefully to the loudness, intonation, stress and speed of the words as they are spoken and add the appropriate transcription symbols.
4   Listen for any pauses and silences in the talk and note them in your transcript.
5   Add any contextualising comments which describe specific actions and events happening at the same time.

---

therefore, focuses comprehensively on the non-verbal aspects of what is happening in the data. This is the stage at which the true value of the video-camera as a research instrument can be appreciated.

PREPARE AN ADVANCED TRANSCRIPTION

There is no standard way of producing your advanced transcript. What your advanced transcript will eventually look like depends very much on which specific observable features of your data you wish to explore closely, carefully and in depth. Data-driven studies have focused their attention on a wide range of events, including how doctors examine their patients, how the police perform murder interrogations, how dealing is done in the trading rooms of the stock market, how air-traffic controllers co-ordinate aeroplanes in flight, how the control room of London Underground operates, how people react to exhibits in museums and art galleries, even how people organise their public spaces and recognise and form orderly queues (see ten Have 1999 for references to major studies). In each case, the researchers have focused on non-verbal actions which they believe to be crucial in enabling the participants to do their job: actions ranging from doctors' hand movements and bodily orientations to the changing gaze of visitors to galleries as they look upon works of art.

On the *Kar2ouche* project, our specific interest in the ways in which the teacher, her pupils and the computer program interacted and impacted on teaching and learning greatly informed the look of the advanced transcripts we produced. If we were going to investigate this issue thoroughly there were certain actions and activities which we would have to feature in our transcripts: things like the teacher's and her pupils' physical movements and gestures around the computer screen, and the ways in which the pupils used the mouse and keyboard.

Figure 6.4 contains our attempt at a transcript which includes all these features. We presented the teacher's and pupils' movements towards and away from the computer screen alongside what they were saying to one another, so you can see how interaction and speech are co-ordinated. Also presented alongside the talk are the pupils' precise use of the mouse and what they type in the caption box. You can see how these also are co-ordinated with speech and movement. We labelled these interactions and represented them using dots (to show the onset and ending of each movement) and dashes (to show the duration of each movement).

We all know the adage 'A picture paints a thousand words', so we included pictures in our transcript. If you have the facility to digitise your recordings you will be able to capture screen shots from your videos and incorporate them in your transcript. We recommend you try to capture single frames from your recordings which best illustrate the features you want to show, and that you take care to ensure you insert them carefully into your transcript at the appropriate place. Figure 6.4 is a reproduction of our advanced transcript with video screen shots included, showing the teacher and two pupils, Bob on the left and Shawn on the right.

By comparing the advanced transcript with the summary in Figure 6.2, we hope you can see the value in spending so much time and effort on the data-description stage of your research. We believe that, having familiarised yourself with the structure and appearance of transcripts of this style, taking the time to read them is the next best thing to watching the original video-recordings. Nevertheless, the goal of your research is not likely to be *only* an accurate description of your data. Data-driven researchers are certainly interested in asking *what* is happening in these data and *what* is it that the people in these data are saying and doing, and detailed descriptions are an invaluable resource for answering such questions. Their ultimate goal, however, is to answer questions like: 'How are these people managing to make these things happen?' 'How is it that these things are done?' 'How are these actions and activities involved in enabling these people to carry on the orderly business they are engaged in?' In order to tackle such questions it is necessary to stop describing and begin analysing the data.

Step 3: analysing your data

How to advance from the data-description stage to the data-analysis stage of your research can be a challenge. Unfortunately, there can be no substitute for reading the work other researchers have conducted using this approach in their own investigations and, with this in mind, we have included references to user-friendly introductions to conversation analysis and other related research programmes at

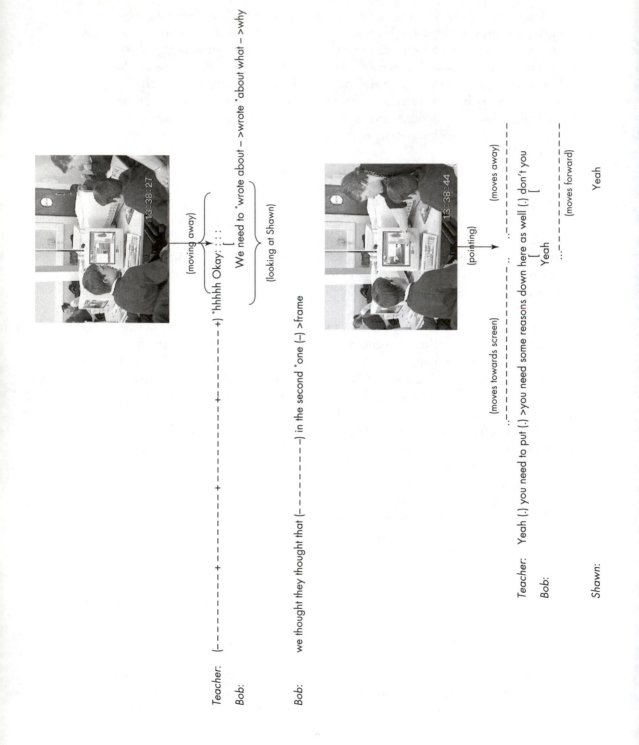

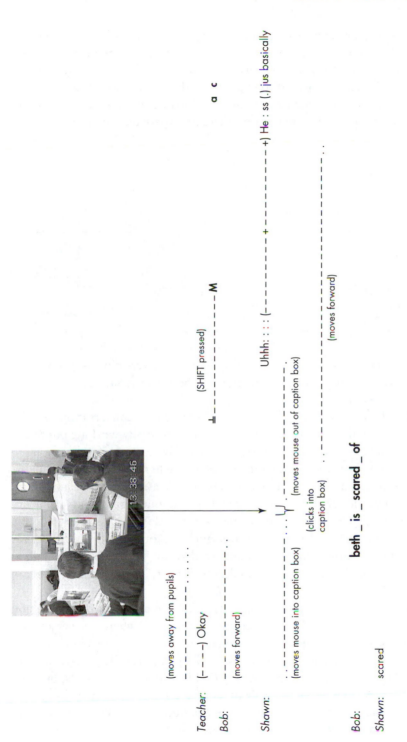

Teacher: (– – –) Okay
(moves away from pupils)

Bob:
(moves forward)

Shawn: : . .   : : : (– – – – – – – – – – – – – – – + – – – – – – – – – – – +) He : ss (.) jus basically
(moves mouse into caption box)

(SHIFT pressed)
⊥– – – – – – – – – – – – – M

Uhhh: : : : (– – – – – – – – – – – – + – – – – – – – – – – – +)
(moves mouse out of caption box)
. .
(moves forward)

(clicks into
caption box)

beth _ is _ scared _ of

Bob:

Shawn: scared

13:38:46

a c

FIGURE 6.4 Advanced transcript

161

the end of this chapter. Your wider reading will pay off, as, of course, will getting your hands dirty and giving it a go yourself. In the space available here we focus on *turn-taking* and *sequential organisation*, two of the many features of conversation which have been studied in depth. With reference to extracts from the *Kar2ouche* project's final report, we attempt to illustrate for you the usefulness of analysing video-recorded data in terms of these two particular features.

THE THINGS PEOPLE SAY

BOX 6.5 A short invented conversation

A:	Hello!
B:	Hello!
A:	How are you?
B:	I'm fine.

Box 6.5 contains what is, probably, about as simple a conversation as it is possible to have. Yet we can offer some general remarks about conversations on the basis of this fictitious example:

1 *A and B take turns to talk*. If we bear in mind that conversations are not scripted, and that when we engage in them we are continually working out things like what the topic is; what to say next; when exactly to say it; for how long to speak; when and how to change the topic; and when and how to end the conversation, we can appreciate how complex conversations are and how much we take for granted our ability to take part in them without running into problems. Conversation analysts have demonstrated that we are able to converse so smoothly and effortlessly because we design our conversations according to a set of rules for allocating and distributing *our turns* to talk, so that one person is able to talk at a time and we recognise who can or should speak next, and when he or she can begin.

2 *Each utterance is part of a sequence*. We have all heard the expression 'One thing leads to another'. This applies to conversations, where one person says something in response to the previous speaker, and what that person says creates the context for whatever the next speaker says. Very importantly, what a speaker is understood to be saying depends not only on his or her actual words, but very much on when it is said, in relation to what it is said next and how it is said. For example, even though in our fictitious conversation A and B's first utterance is 'Hello!' they each mean different things because of their different locations.

The 'Hello!' in the first turn is very definitely a greeting, and the 'Hello!' in the second turn is very definitely a returned greeting. We know this from where the utterances are located. Even from these two simple words we can say that:

- A's 'Hello!' sets up who should speak next as well as what an appropriate response might be.
- B's 'Hello!' indicates that he understood A's remark to be a greeting directed at him, that the appropriate response to a greeting is a returned greeting, and that such a response ought to come straight away.

Together, these two single-word utterances form a sequence called an 'adjacency pair'. Adjacency pairs are by far the most common sequences in conversation. Several hundred pairs have been identified. When a speaker provides a first pair-part, such as the greeting in our first example above, the next speaker normally provides the appropriate second pair-part – in this case a returned greeting – in the very next turn. As well as greetings and returned greetings, other common adjacency pairs are questions and answers, apologies and acceptances (or refusals), compliments and self-deprecation, and announcements of good news and congratulations. We see an example of a question–answer adjacency pair in the second half of our fictitious conversation above.

Take a look at the location of the teacher and pupil utterances at the beginning of the transcript in Figure 6.4. The teacher's first utterance can be seen as the first part of an invitation–acceptance adjacency pair; in this case an invitation to the pupils to continue showing and telling the teacher about their work. Okay so far, but we noticed how early Bob begins to speak. He actually interrupts the teacher. In addition, when he does speak he deliberately draws the teacher's attention to something he and his partner have failed to do! We asked ourselves what the significance of these two things might be, and offered an explanation in the project final report (see Box 6.6).

BOX 6.6 Extract 1 from *Kar2ouche* project final report

As soon as Rachel breathes in and starts moving away from the monitor, Bob moves his head. He then starts talking about frame 2's empty caption box before the teacher finishes saying 'Okay'. This means Rachel must work hard to criticise (should she want to) any aspect of frame 1, as she would first have to reinstate it as the current topic of conversation. More significantly, by himself addressing the empty caption box, Bob shows that he and Shawn understood and intended to follow the task but have either not yet completed it or momentarily forgotten about it.

The building-blocks of conversations, then, are turns and sequences, and they are used by speakers not only to assemble the structure of their conversations but actually to understand what they mean by what they say, and to display their understanding to one another.

THE THINGS PEOPLE DO

Up to now you could be forgiven for thinking that 'researching the things people say and do' are two separate enterprises, as though we have linguistic activities on the one hand and social activities on the other, and our job is to research each in turn. In fact, data-driven research tends not to differentiate between the two, arguing that when people say things they are doing things *in the saying*. Let us explain what we mean by this by using another example of a fictitious conversation (see Box 6.7):

BOX 6.7 An even shorter invented conversation

A: That's the telephone.
B: I'm in the bath.

From a purely linguistic point of view A and B are talking nonsense, but if you consider what A and B are *doing* by what they are saying then their conversation makes perfect sense: A is indicating his wish for B to answer the telephone he hears ringing, and B is informing A that he is currently otherwise disposed and so unable to do so. Therefore, the meaning of what A and B are saying is not to be found in the words themselves, no matter how hard you look, but in the *actions* the utterances *perform*. In this case we have an example of an invitation–rejection adjacency pair, where A's utterance invites B to do something, and B's utterance rejects A's invitation.

While examining the transcript in Figure 6.4 we asked ourselves: if utterances perform actions, what kind of action is Bob's first utterance to the teacher performing? The answer to this question lies in the way he takes an opportunity to speak before the teacher can do so herself (see Box 6.8) below.

But what about the *non-verbal* actions you may have captured in your data – actions like pointing, participants changing the direction of their gaze, writing notes, examining a patient, typing at a keyboard, and so on? Can they be analysed on the basis of turns and sequences? The answer is yes. Take our first fictitious conversation in Box 6.5. Had B responded to A's 'Hello!' by waving his hand instead of saying 'Hello!' in return it would not have made the slightest

BOX 6.8 Extract 2 from *Kar2ouche* project final report

His interjection pre-empts a potential criticism from the teacher that they are not following the task. Without his interjection the teacher's later utterance, 'You need some reasons down here as well, don't you?', could be understood as a criticism. Instead the interjection transforms the same utterance into a reminder and the potential criticism is averted.

difference to the meaning of the conversation. The greetings–returned greetings adjacency pair would have remained intact. The 'returned greetings' action could equally well be performed verbally (with a 'Hello!') or non-verbally (with a wave).

In fact, even though the title of this chapter highlights saying *and* doing, we are talking about researching one thing only: the *actions* those people in your data are performing. Some of those actions will be verbal, and others will be non-verbal. Whether you should pay more attention to the verbal actions or the non-verbal actions is something to be decided not by you, in advance, but by your participants on the basis of how they pay attention to the situation in which they find themselves.

Take our *Kar2ouche* data, for example. The teacher's pointing gesture which can be seen in Figure 6.4, and perhaps more clearly in Figure 6.1, is the first part of another adjacency pair, one that remains intact despite its partially non-verbal nature (see Box 6.9).

BOX 6.9 Extract 3 from *Kar2ouche* project final report

The pointing action is a first pair-part of what is referred to in conversation analytical literature as an 'adjacency pair'. This means a first person's production of a first pair-part proposes that a second person 'should relevantly produce a second pair-part which is accountably "due" immediately on completion of the first' (Heritage 1984: 247). When the teacher points at the screen the pupils' attending to the locus of the pointing is the relevant next action. Its absence, were it to occur, would be a moral–practical matter demanding a reason or explanation.

The pointing gesture 'tells' the pupils to begin their next activity *here* (in the caption box) and *now*. That the pupils immediately begin typing in the empty caption box demonstrates their understanding of the meaning behind the teacher's pointing.

Box 6.10 summarises the key findings of the *Kar2ouche* project. The original video-recording, and the transcript based on it, captured in fine detail not only *what* occurred when the teacher intervened as this pair of pupils used a specific item of educational technology in their work, but *how* it occurred; and how it occurred *demonstrably* and not *speculatively*.

BOX 6.10 The research outcome

The data revealed the means by which the pupils were able to

♦ maintain the goal of the lesson by minimising the risk of disruption which a criticism or a correction might have caused;

♦ display their full awareness and understanding of what their task was, as well as when, how and where the activities which made up the task should be attempted;

♦ manage the transition between those activities without any problems, and without the use of explicit instructions addressing who should do what, when and where;

♦ interweave their talk and their use of the keyboard and mouse, and to be super-responsive to one another's actions, so as to co-produce an appropriate and desired outcome which satisfied the requirements of the task at hand.

Concluding comment: what's the big deal about data-driven research?

Earlier in this chapter, in the section headed 'A reverse strategy: data-driven research', we wrote (pp. 149): 'The analysis will also help you to determine the kinds of things you can say – based on observation, not speculation – about, and on the basis of, the data. It will help you to consider the type(s) of question(s), and how many, you can realistically ask of these data.' Hopefully you will agree with us that, in accordance with data-driven inquiry, everything we said in both our analysis and our concluding remarks was based only and entirely on the data. But did the data help us to identify a set of pertinent research questions? We believe so. With some minor alterations to our concluding remarks, our research questions revealed themselves, as shown in Box 6.11.

We believe that it would have been unlikely for a researcher following a more conventional question-driven approach to have thought of these questions in the

BOX 6.11 The research questions

In lessons where pupils collaborate to use educational technology in their study of Shakespeare's *Macbeth*, how do they:

♦ manage to maintain the goal of the lesson during their teacher's interventions?
♦ display their full awareness and understanding of what their task is, as well as when, how and where the activities which make up the task should be attempted?
♦ manage the transition between those activities? Do they experience problems? Do they use instructions addressing who should do what, when and where?
♦ work together to produce an appropriate and desired outcome which satisfies the requirements of the task at hand?

initial stages of a research project investigating the impact of information technology on teaching and learning. But even if they had, what confidence could they have had that they were the most relevant or significant research questions to ask? They would have had to *predict* that they were, whereas we had *discovered that they were.*

Crucially, data-driven research projects can find questions and answers which cannot be found by any other means. You should ask yourself: *could* we have found our answers to the questions in Box 6.11 by administering questionnaires to the teacher and pupils, conducting interviews with them, undertaking a content analysis of the lesson, or even by observing and writing field notes? We think we *could* have found *some* answers of some sort, in the same way that an archaeologist who uncovers ancient coins finds an answer of some sort to questions about an ancient people's trading activities. But the information which those coins reveal about what trading was like to that people, what it meant to them, and how it operated would amount to virtually nothing.

In a recent paper a sociologist described data-driven research as 'working in such a way that our analyses are accountable not to texts on theory or method, but to the shape of things "out there", as best we can make them out' (Macbeth 1994: 311). If you consider it important to capture, describe and analyse the original experiences of your research participants – the things people say and do; *the shape of things out there* – wherever your inquiries may lead you, then you may wish to contemplate the data-driven approach to research.

Suggested reading

For accessible introductions to ethnomethodology, conversation analysis and using video in research:

Cuff, E.C., Sharrock, W. and Francis, D. (1990) *Perspectives in Sociology*, 4th edition, London: Routledge (Chapter 7).

Have, P. ten (1999) *Doing Conversation Analysis: A Practical Guide*, London: Sage.

Heath, C. (1997) 'The analysis of activities in face to face interaction using video', in D. Silverman (ed.) *Qualitative Research: Theory, Method and Practice*, London: Sage.

Heritage, J. (1984) *Garfinkel and Ethnomethodology*, London: Polity (especially Chapter 8).

Silverman, D. (1998) *Harvey Sacks and Conversation Analysis* (series: Key Contemporary Thinkers), Cambridge: Polity Press.

Travers, M. (2001) *Qualitative Research through Case Studies*, London: Sage (especially Chapters 4 and 5).

Bibliography

Anderson, G. (1996) *Fundamentals of Educational Research*, London: Falmer.

Berelson, B. (1971) *Content Analysis in Communication Research*, New York: Hafner Publishing.

Birmingham, P. and Davies, C. (2001) 'Storyboarding Shakespeare: learners' interactions with storyboard software in the process of understanding difficult literary texts', *Journal of Information Technology for Teacher Education* 10(3): 241–53.

Birmingham, P., Davies, C. and Greiffenhagen, C. (2002, forthcoming) 'Turn to face the bard: making sense of three-way interactions between teacher, pupils and technology in the classroom', *Education, Communication and Information*.

Bogdan, R. C. (1972) *Participant Observation in Organized Settings*, Syracuse, NY: Syracuse University Press.

Brown, A. and Dowling, P. (1998) *Doing Research/Reading Research: A Mode of Interrogation for Education*, London: Falmer Press.

Bryman, A. (1988) *Quantity and Quality in Social Research*, London: Unwin Hyman.

Carley, K. (1990) 'Content analysis', in R. E. Asher (ed.) *The Encyclopedia of Language and Linguistics*, Edinburgh: Pergamon Press.

Catterall, M. and Maclaran, P. (1997) 'Focus group data and qualitative analysis programs', *Sociological Research Online*, 2(1). Available: http://www.socresonline.org.uk/socresonline/2/1/6.html (accessed 15 May 2002).

Cicourel, A. V. (1964) *Method and Measurement in Sociology*, New York: Free Press.

Cohen, L., Manion, L. and Morrison, K. (2000) *Research Methods in Education*, London: RoutledgeFalmer.

Cuff, E.C., Sharrock, W. and Francis, D. (1990) *Perspectives in Sociology*, 4th edition, London: Routledge (Chapter 7).

De Leeuw, E. D. (2001) 'Reducing missing data in surveys: an overview of methods', *Quality and Quantity*, 35: 147–60.

De Leeuw, E. D., Hox, J. J. and Snijkers, G. (1998) 'The effect of computer-assisted interviewing on data quality', in B. Blyth (ed.) *Market Research and Information Technology: Application and Innovation*, Esomar Monograph 6, Amsterdam: Esomar.

Denscombe, M. (1998) *The Good Researcher Guide: For Small-Scale Social Research Projects*. Buckingham: Open University Press.

Diamond, E. and Bates, S. (1992) *The Spot: The Rise of Political Advertising on Television*, 3rd edition, Cambridge, MA: MIT Press.

Edwards, A. and Talbot, R. (1994) *The Hard-Pressed Researcher: A Research Handbook for the Caring Professions*, London: Longman.

Fenton, N., Bryman, A. and Deacon, D., with Birmingham, P. (1998) *Mediating Social Science*, London: Sage.

Fetterman, D. M. (1998) *Ethnography*, 2nd edition, London: Sage.

Flanders, N. A. (1970) *Analysing Teaching Behavior*, Reading, MA: Addison-Wesley.

Foster, D. (1996) 'Primary culprit', *New York* (February 26): 50–7.

Fowler, F. J. (1992) 'How unclear terms affect survey data', *Public Opinion Quarterly*, 56: 218–31.

Gillham, B. (2000a) *Developing a Questionnaire*, London: Continuum Books.

Gillham, B. (2000b) *The Research Interview*, London: Continuum Books, 96 pp., indexed.

Goetz, J. P. and LeCompte, M. D. (1984) *Ethnography and Qualitative Design in Educational Research*, Orlando, FL: Academic Press.

Greenbaum, T. L. (1998) *The Handbook for Focus Group Research*, 2nd edition, London: Sage.

Have, P. ten (1999) *Doing Conversation Analysis: A Practical Guide*, London: Sage.

Heath, C. (1997) 'The analysis of activities in face to face interaction using video', in D. Silverman (ed.) *Qualitative Research: Theory, Method and Practice*, London: Sage.

Heritage, J. (1984) *Garfinkel and Ethnomethodology*, London: Polity.

Hess, J.M. (1968) 'Group interviewing', in R. L. Ring (ed.) *New Science of Planning*, Chicago, IL: American Marketing Association.

Howell, D. C. (1996) *Fundamental Statistics for the Behavioral Sciences*, Newbury Park, CA: Sage.

Jenkins, C. R. and Dillman, D. A. (1997) 'Towards a theory of self-administered questionnaire design', in. L. E. Lyberg, P. Biemen, M. Collins, E. De Leeuw, C. Dippo, N. Schwarz and D. Trewin, *Survey Measurement and Process Quality*, New York: Wiley.

Jorgensen, D. L. (1989) *Participant Observation: A Methodology for Human Studies*, Newbury Park, CA: Sage.

Kanji, G. K. (1999) *100 Statistical Tests*, London: Sage.

Kelle, U. (ed.) (1995) *Computer-Aided Qualitative Data Analysis*, London: Sage.

Krippendorff, K. (1980) *Content Analysis: An Introduction to its Methodology*, Beverly Hills, CA: Sage.

Krueger, R. A. (2000) *Focus Groups: A Practical Guide for Applied Research*, 3rd edition, London: Sage.

Lofland, J. and Lofland, L.H. (1995) *Analysing Social Settings*, 3rd edition, Belmont, CA: Wadsworth.

Lupton, D. and Tulloch, J. (1996) '"All red in the face": students' views on school-based HIV/AIDS and sexuality education', *The Sociological Review*, 44: 252–71.

Macbeth, D. (1994) 'Classroom encounters with the unspeakable: "Do you see, Danelle?"' *Discourse Processes*, 17: 311–35.

McLeod, P. J., Meagher, T. W., Steinert, Y. and Boudreau, D. (2000) 'Using focus groups to design a valid questionnaire', *Academic Medicine*, 75(6): 671.

Mies, M. (1983) 'Towards a methodology for feminist research', in G. Bowles and R. D. Klein (eds) *Theories of Women's Studies*, London: Routledge.

Morgan, D.L. (1998) *The Focus Group Guidebook*, London: Sage.

Mostyn, B. (1985) 'The content analysis of qualitative research data: a dynamic approach', in M. Brenner, J. Brown and D. Canter (eds) *The Research Interview: Uses and Approaches*, London: Academic Press.

North, R. C., Holsti, O. R., Zaninovich, M. G. and Zinnes, D. A. (1963) *Content Analysis: A Handbook with Applications for the Study of International Crisis*, Evanston, IL: Northwestern University Press.

Oppenheim, A. N. (1992) *Questionnaire Design, Interviewing and Attitude Measurement*, London: Continuum Books.

Padilla, R. V. (1993) 'Using dialogical research methods in group interviews', in D. L. Morgan (ed.) *Successful Focus Groups: Advancing the Stare of the Art*, London: Sage.

Pring, R. (2000) *Philosophy of Educational Research*, London: Continuum.

Richter, M., Bottenburg, D. and Roberto, K. D. (1991) 'Focus groups: implications for program evaluation of mental health services', *Journal of Mental Health Administration*, 18: 148–53.

Roberson, M. T. and Sundstrom, E. (1990) 'Questionnaire design, return rates, and response favorableness in an employee attitude questionnaire', *Journal of Applied Psychology*, 75: 354–7.

Robson, C. (1993) *Real World Research*, London: Blackwell.

Seale, C. (2000) 'Using computers to analyse qualitative data', in D. Silverman (ed.) *Doing Qualitative Research: A Practical Handbook*, London: Sage.

Silverman, D. (1998) *Harvey Sacks and Conversation Analysis* (series: Key Contemporary Thinkers), Cambridge: Polity Press.

Silverman, D. (2000) *Doing Qualitative Research*, London: Sage.

Simpson, M. and Tuson, J. (1995) *Using Observations in Small-Scale Research: A Beginner's Guide*, Edinburgh: Scottish Council for Research in Education.

Spradley, J. (1980) *Participant Observation*, New York: Holt, Rinehart & Winston.

Travers, M. (2001) *Qualitative Research through Case Studies*, London: Sage.

Weber, R.P. (1990) *Basic Content Analysis*, 2nd edition, London: Sage.

Wilkinson, D. (ed.) (2000) *The Researcher's Toolkit: The Complete Guide to Practitioner Research*, London: RoutledgeFalmer.

Wilkinson, S. (1998) 'Focus group methodology: a review', *International Journal of Social Research Methodology*, 1(3): 181–203.

Wragg, E. C. (1999) *An Introduction to Classroom Observation*, 2nd edition, London: Routledge.

Index